I WILL ALWAYS BE WITH YOU

By
Tracey Britz

Grosvenor House
Publishing Limited

All rights reserved
Copyright © Tracey Britz, 2025
The right of Tracey Britz to be identified as the author of this
work has been asserted in accordance with Section 78
of the Copyright, Designs and Patents Act 1988

The book cover is copyright to Tracey Britz

This book is published by
Grosvenor House Publishing Ltd
Link House
140 The Broadway, Tolworth, Surrey, KT6 7HT.
www.grosvenorhousepublishing.co.uk

This book is sold subject to the conditions that it shall not, by way of
trade or otherwise, be lent, resold, hired out or otherwise circulated
without the author's or publisher's prior consent in any form of
binding or cover other than that in which it is published and
without a similar condition including this condition being imposed
on the subsequent purchaser.

A CIP record for this book
is available from the British Library

ISBN 978-1-83615-177-7
eBook ISBN 978-1-83615-178-4

My name is Tracey Britz. This book is about a chapter in my life story that was long and hard. However, going through this challenging period is testimony to how I discovered what real faith is, learning that God is wonderful, and nothing is impossible if we believe. With God all things are possible.

I also learnt that we can't always rely on people in this world, as they will always disappoint us in some way. But God will always be there and help us through situations—even when we feel alone, lost and when there is no hope.

This journey has taken about 8 years so far and is still ongoing.

On the way, there have been a lot of people and situations that have played a big part in getting me to where I am today. I am grateful to each one, for I know now that it was all done to help me, no matter how big or small.

This is my own experience and my own opinions on my life journey.

I hope that by reading this book, you will see that we are never alone, that things don't always happen the way we want them to, but in the end, things still work out, no matter how hard it may be at the time.

Everything that happens makes us stronger and helps our faith grow, and it makes us realise that there is much more to life than we think—even if it doesn't always feel that way.

Most importantly, we are never alone—even when it feels like we are. All we need to do is hold on; Jesus is with us and will never leave us nor forsake us, no matter what situation you are in.

When you read this book, I would suggest that you put on some instrumental Christian music in the background, or simply put your earphones in and relax as you read.

CONTENTS

The Start of the Journey	1
The Dark Times Roll In	16
Thinking of the End	26
Things Need to Get Better	33
Things Started to Get Better	41
Let the Years Roll On	49
Changes	58
Keeping the Faith	64
A New Year	68
Here We Go Again	82
The Beginning of the Worst Time of My Life	92
My Dream	113
Moving on Slowly	121
Delays	129
New Beginnings	144
Already Another New Year	153
Coming to an End	170

The Start of the Journey

My husband and I thought that our lives were good. We both had good jobs and we had a daughter who was beautiful, a real gift from God. We were not wealthy, and we were not poor; we always just had enough, and we were happy.

As it happens, we did have a lot of debts, but we were slowly working through this, and we thought that we had a good relationship with God. We thought our faith was in a good place, and that we understood what it meant.

However, as things in South Africa were changing quickly for the worse, we started to think that we needed to consider leaving our country to ensure that we could give our daughter the best chance in life, and to keep her safe.

What I mean by changing for the worse, is that finding a job and keeping it was getting harder; the cost of living was getting higher; and just walking to the shop or driving down the road was no longer safe. For my husband, our safety was the main worry, as he worked out of the country for long periods.

Now you might ask about safety. Well, our house was in a security complex. This meant that there were high walls around all the properties, with electric fencing around as well. In addition, we had security cameras monitoring the front door and back garden; every door had an additional metal security gate fitted on it; every window was covered with huge metal bars; and every opening window had bars in it too. This was to try and keep us safe from people attempting to break in. It felt like we lived in a prison.

When I was younger, children could play in the streets, you could walk to the shops with no worries, and play outside with your friends, but now things have changed drastically. Nowadays, if the children play outside, you can't leave them alone, as they can be abducted in the blink of an eye. Walking to the shop, you have to continuously keep looking around to see if there are any suspicious people looking at you, or to check that you are not being followed. Not only that, you have to be careful when passing big bushes or shrubs, as you never know if someone is hiding in them, or behind them, waiting for you to pass so that they can attack you from behind.

Yes, I know that not everyone may have felt like this, but this is what it felt like for me.

A few years before, my husband had studied hard and obtained an engineering qualification at an Australian institute. He was now working in the mining industry.

When we considered leaving South Africa, we thought that as he had an Australian qualification, this would open a door for us to be able to go to Australia. However, the visa costs involved and what we had to do just to qualify for an Australia visa seemed out of reach.

However, we thought that we would not let money stop us, so we tried and kept pushing to start the process. It was slow, but we felt like it was the right thing to do. At that time we also thought that Australia was the right country to go to. We thought that this was what God's plan was for us, and we knew we would just have to work hard to make it possible.

WE HAD NO IDEA WHAT LAY AHEAD OF US AT THIS TIME!

The process for the Australian visa was difficult. There were many different requirements that had to be met, and as my husband worked away most of the time, we just seemed to be getting nowhere. We then found out that God had blessed us with a son. My daughter at this time was 5 years old, so our plans to leave the country had to be put on hold as we prepared for a new family member. At the time, we thought that maybe Jesus didn't want us to leave the country then. We thought maybe we still had something that we had to do—or that we had to help someone.

Shortly after knowing that I was pregnant, things started changing in South Africa. They seemed to be getting even worse. The mining industry was starting to slow down and there were problems with investors. Because of this, the mines were putting a hold on all new projects and work was slowing down.

Nine months later we welcomed our wonderful son into the family. At this time, we were still doing okay. However, as work in the mining industry had slowed down completely, my husband's working hours were being restricted and he was earning slightly less (but we were surviving).

My husband started hearing stories about the company he was working for: that it was not doing very well, that they were going to start making changes, and that this would start with making people redundant as part of restructuring the company. We didn't know if it was all true at this stage, as this was one of the biggest mining companies in South Africa and had contracts all over the world.

The project my husband was working on at the time was still going forward and they said that there was plenty of work to go around, that he should not worry, and that not everything that had been said was true.

Then a few months later, the company started making redundancies, projects were being stopped or cancelled, the number of people working on projects was being reduced and working times were being cut further.

Due to all the uncertainty, my husband started looking for other work, talking to people he knew who had their own companies. They all said that if he found himself without a job, they would take him on. We thought that this was good to know, that there were a few options if things did go wrong and my husband lost his job.

Then one day the news came that the project my husband was on was finishing and he would have to return to the office. At the time they said we should not worry, as there were other projects in the pipeline. They wanted to have him involved in design, which my husband was happy about as he always wanted to work in this division.

Things were looking good. He was enjoying the design work and over the months all the feedback he received was great. However, once again the rumours started: that if you were in the office and used to be a person who worked away on projects, you had a target on your back for being on the redundancy list. When this started, my husband again spoke to people who said not to worry because if he needed a job, they would take him on. He also started looking for work again, but not one job he applied for came through—not even an interview.

Things started getting worse quickly in his company. It was becoming really worrying. When my husband's work became office-based, his former salary had been halved. Because of this, general living was getting a lot harder for us, as we'd been so used to the higher salary he'd earned for years before.

My husband told me one day that he knew that he would be called in to see the manager soon for a chat. I asked if he had been told something, to which he said no. But he also said he thought he could see it coming as he'd heard rumours in the office.

Then one day when I was at work only a few weeks later, my husband called me to say that he had been told to attend a meeting with the head of the department later that day. I tried to suggest that it might be about another project, or to discuss the work he was doing in the office, as I felt it was important for us both to keep thinking of positive outcomes, not negative ones. (I was always like that, trying my best not to think of the worst.)

Unfortunately, a few hours later my husband called me again. It had been the meeting we both didn't want. He was being made redundant. I think we'd both known it was coming, but at the same time we'd hoped it wouldn't.

I am aware there will be many people reading this who know how it feels to get this sort of news, but if you have never had this happen, I will try to explain.

When my husband phoned me back after his meeting, I was standing in the car park. On hearing bad news, in that moment you feel nothing. You don't think of anything, you are just stunned. But then realisation comes in a huge wave, bringing worry, sadness, thoughts about money, family, work, bills, heartbreak, so you can't breathe. You feel like you are falling, and everything is collapsing around you in one second. You have all these feelings, and you don't even know how you are going to make it through that moment. You then tell yourself to try not to panic, but this is not as easy as it may sound. Just as you try taking a breath to calm down, all the feelings and thoughts come rushing back again, and you feel sick and overwhelmed with different feelings.

You want to cry as your heart breaks, but at the same time you want to scream, shout, or hit something out of anger. I had to pull myself together as I had to go back and work. I had to put on an act like nothing was wrong, but in the back of my mind all I could think was, what is going to happen now?

The rest of the day was a blur, but on my way home, I knew that no matter what it looked like or how I felt, I had to keep positive for my family. I then remembered that people had told my husband they could help him with work, so we didn't have to be worried; all we had to do was contact them.

My husband started sending out his CV and contacting the people that had offered him work before, but we quickly realised that most of the people were just big talkers and could not actually help my husband with a job.

Slowly, all those feelings and worries were creeping back in, and if someone said something like, 'How are you?' or looked at me, all I wanted to do was cry. But at the same time, I would say to myself, 'You can't fall apart, you can't let people know', so I would bite back the tears and all the feelings that I could feel running through me, and put a smile on, like there were no problems at all.

My son's first birthday was my husband's last day in his job. We had already arranged a party with our family months before for that Saturday, so we couldn't change it. The whole day we tried to act as if nothing was wrong in front of all the family, as we didn't want anyone to really know about our situation. They all knew that my husband had been made redundant, but they had no idea that my husband was battling to find work.

I know that there are many people who understand what we do and what it means to hide things from people: you put on a mask for the day and act as if there are no worries, act like everything is perfect while deep down inside you are sick from worry and wish you could just sit in a corner and not have to fake a smile or a laugh. You silently wish that you could break down and cry your heart out all day.

That following week, my husband contacted the other people who had always said they would have work for him, but their stories were different again. They would say, 'Send us your CV' or 'We'll see what we can do' or

'There are no openings.' And these were friends who had their own companies, who had always promised him work. Now, when he really needed their help, he quickly realised it was all lies and big talk.

I can just imagine how my husband must have felt during this time. He must have felt like a fool, having trusted these people, and felt useless, demoralised, hurt, let down and confused all at the same time. Then over and above this, there were all the worries about what was going to happen and how he was going to provide for his family.

We knew that all companies were going through hard times, and understood that it was tough for everyone, however I thought that people should have just told my husband the truth at the start and not given my husband false hope or confidence that they could help when this was clearly not the case.

Within the first week that my husband didn't have work, it felt like everything was going to fall apart. We knew we had some savings, and we knew we could get through a few months on this, but once funds had run out...? We knew that my salary could not cover our monthly expenses and living costs.

We tried hard not to let the worries get us down, we prayed and tried to keep positive, but every day that passed it became harder and harder. The negative thoughts and feelings just kept coming and making us feel worse and more and more worried.

As the first month passed, the stress and worries built up as my husband couldn't find any work. He had sent his CV to hundreds of places, but not even one reply or one interview came from it. I tried to keep my husband thinking positively and we tried to keep everything positive in front of the children and the rest of the family.

My husband's younger sister had work on and off; his mother lived with her and looked after her three children. It was hard for his mother, but at the same time she was helping someone so that she could work without having to worry about childcare and the associated costs.

When my husband did have a job, he'd always tried to help his mother and younger sister, and her children, as they were always battling with money situations. For example, we would buy their groceries for the month and send them money when we could. But when my husband lost his job, we had to say that we could no longer help them as much as we had before. At first, they were understanding, but after a month of saying no and sorry we can't help with food or money, they became so mean to my husband. His sister would say he had a duty to help his mother. And he would have done, if he could have. But we had our own family and responsibilities that we had to deal with at the time, and it just seemed that they didn't even think of this. His sister would keep saying his mother was ill and needed medicine, or that her children had no food.

I would get so angry about this. My husband was already stressed with not having work, and not being able to find work, and we were also struggling to keep our family going with food and basics. So we could do without his younger sister nagging and saying how terrible he was because he was not giving her money. They had no idea how it hurt my husband that he couldn't help them. They never thought about his feelings and what he was going through. And even if I tried to explain our situation to them and why we couldn't help, they wouldn't listen, or were not interested in what I had to say.

HOW COULD THEY BE SO BLIND NOT TO SEE WHAT HE WAS GOING THROUGH?

I know in hard situations people can be desperate, and say things without thinking, but it was every day that they would do this to him. This made me extremely angry, as they upset him daily, so my heart hardened against them.

There were a few times before when we were helping them that I had suggested to my husband that we should stop giving his younger sister money and food because she was getting so used to us providing for them that it was expected all the time. At the same time, my husband's older sister and husband were also helping them out with money and food, so they actually didn't have to buy much or try and know how to budget well, as we were all there providing for them.

At that time, my husband would get angry with me for saying we shouldn't constantly help them. He would say it was his mother and younger sister and he had the money to help, so he would. However, now I wish I had been harder on him and pushed him more not to help them, as maybe then they would not have been so horrible to him now that he wasn't able to help them anymore.

I know you are probably thinking that I am a terrible person not wanting to help a family in need, but you know that gut feeling you get when you know that something just doesn't seem right… well, I'd had this feeling for years that the money we were giving them was not going for food or rent, that it was just being wasted on other things. I didn't know what, but I knew there was something else going on. I hope you will now understand why I said we shouldn't help as much; something just felt wrong.

When they didn't understand that we were not in a position to help, my husband spoke to his mother to try and explain. She would tell him not to worry and that she understood. But then a day later, his younger sister would say hurtful things to him such as, how could he not help with his mother's medicine, as she was ill and in pain. But when he had spoken to his mother earlier, she had been fine and didn't need medicine. This behaviour confirmed my suspicions, that the money we used to give his sister was spent on other things, and because of that, she treated him like a piece of rubbish, as she obviously couldn't get whatever it was that she wanted anymore.

The months and days kept passing. We had reached the stage where our savings had run out, and we knew from that next month we would not be able to pay for our house, our cars, and most of our bills. However, we tried to stay positive, as my husband had been for two interviews, and we were just waiting to hear back from one of them.

The waiting time felt like forever, finally, my husband received a call with a job offer. He would have to work out of the country again. It was on a contact basis again. And the money would not be as much as he'd earned before, but due to our situation, he had to take the job. As the saying goes, 'Beggars can't be choosers, and anything, is better than nothing.'

My husband started his new job and it seemed to be okay. Unfortunately, as the money he earned was a lot less than he'd earned before, in the months that followed, we fell behind on paying our bills, as we could not cover all the costs.

We knew we couldn't keep stalling on payments, so we started making plans with payment breaks, or payment plans with different companies. Some companies understood and were willing to work with us, and others just didn't care about the situation and were not willing to help. I always thought that a company would be happy to get something rather than nothing. But I was wrong.

The Dark Times Roll In

As I'm sure many of you know, with our financial situation it felt like we were on a slippery slope, as if we were falling down in slow motion. And every day we asked and prayed for it to get better, but this didn't happen.

I knew my husband was breaking inside. He never said it, or showed, it but I knew. If I was feeling down, sad and in despair, and wondering just how much worse things could get, I knew he must be feeling the same. Being a man, he would feel even worse.

A man is meant to be the provider for his family, the head of the home, and for some time now he had not been able to this. Having no work and not earning as much as he had before, he could no longer be the provider he once was, and I knew that this would have been eating away at him and mentally breaking him down.

Things got worse. We had to start planning to sell our things just to have money for food. It felt terrible as we were slowly losing everything, and knew that at the end, if things didn't change, we would end up homeless.

Through all this we had to make sure that our children didn't see what was happening. Our son was a baby and needed all the normal things, like nappies. While my daughter was older, she still needed to attend nursery school so she knew the basics before starting school—which we were now having a hard time paying for.

Every morning on my way to work (when I also dropped off my daughter at nursery school), we sat in traffic for about an hour. One day we heard a song on the radio and for some unknown reason I listened to every word that was sung. Listening to the words, I realised that she was singing no matter how hard things are, we need to have faith, and where was my faith? I thought I had faith, but it was not as strong as I had hoped or thought it was.

During these hard times, we tried to stay positive, and we were praying. But nothing was working.

Everything was getting too much for me. It felt like I had the weight of the world on my shoulders, but I had to act like nothing was wrong in front of the children and everyone else around me. At night when everyone was asleep, I would lie in bed and think of everything that was happening in our lives. This would serve to break me even more and I would start to cry. But I had to cry softly to ensure no one in the house would hear me. And I would pray for help, as I didn't know how much longer we could carry on in this way.

Then, one day sitting in traffic, I was feeling very down, I felt dead inside. Every day was just another day. It felt like I was in a washing machine that was stuck in a very long wash cycle. Then something inside me told me to look around. And there, on the other side of the road, was a huge white truck, on the back of which was written in big red letters, 'TRUST GOD'.

After seeing this, I realised that Jesus was still with us. But there must be something that we were still doing wrong, that he was not happy with and for that reason, he was not helping us. So I tried hard to think about all the things we did and what we needed to change. However, all I could think was that we were trying so hard to do everything right. And I didn't know what else we could do or change to make things better.

As my husband was working and earning an income, we were just trying to play a very hard balancing act with keeping bills paid here and there and having to try and cover the everyday living costs. However, things just kept getting harder, and the costs seemed to keep climbing. One month I knew that if we didn't get a lot of extra money soon, we were going to have a problem. The fear of losing everything and ending up homeless was on the horizon, and there was nothing more we could do.

We had been hanging in there for about a year. My daughter had to start primary school soon, and the school which was near to our house was expensive. We had to pay a huge deposit if we wanted to ensure a place was kept for her. We obviously couldn't afford this.

As we had inquired at the school before, I received a message one day that they had an Open Day. If we attended and put my daughter's name down on the day, we wouldn't have to pay the large deposit just to keep her spot. This was a blessing for us and an answer to one of our prayers. For a moment it seemed that maybe things were going to get better; things might be turning around. However, at the same time we couldn't afford to put my son in nursery school, so he stayed at home with my mother, who looked after him for me. (She had already been living with us for many years.)

At the start of the year my salary increased and I thought for a moment that this would help us. But my daughter had now started primary school and the costs rose because I had a full-time job and my husband worked away, which meant I had to put my daughter in after-school club. I had no choice and just had to do this. At the time I didn't realise this, but God helped us to cover the additional schooling costs with my salary increase. However, as it didn't help us out of the hole we were in at the time, I didn't see that.

One afternoon after work I was on my way to pick up my daughter from after-school club at the new primary school when I stopped at a traffic light and looked in my mirror. I saw a man in a big Land Rover busy on his phone. He didn't look up. And just as I thought to myself, *He is not going to stop*, SMASH! He drove into the back of my car.

It all seemed to happen in slow motion, but at the same time it happened so quickly. The man admitted it was his fault and there was not much damage to my car, so we swapped details and I headed on to collect my daughter, wondering what else could possibly go wrong. I now had to get quotes for repairs, and all I saw were more costs that we could not afford, with additional excesses that had to be paid. I chose not to claim through my insurance but only through the other person's, as he was one hundred per cent at fault. Doing it this way meant that I didn't have to pay any excesses.

Just as the month was coming to an end and I had no idea how we were going to make it through the next month, I received a payment form the third-party insurer. This was a blessing, as we needed the money.

This extra boost helped us a lot, as we could make it stretch. This little time of feeling good, that things might be looking up and changing for the better didn't last long.

It just felt like every day things just kept getting worse, but I kept praying and tried to stay positive. I was trying to cut down on everything, but you get to a point where there is nothing more you can do. As we were becoming more and more desperate, unable to see how things were going to get better, my husband and I started looking again at the option to leave our country—he hated working away and not having a stable job, not knowing when his contract would come to an end (there was no prospect of an extension), and always having this cloud over our heads that things were not improving—but there was nothing we could find. There were companies in other countries that would pay the costs for visas if they employed you, but at that time we couldn't find anything on the job market.

Then there were whispers again that my husband's contract was coming to an end. This just made my heart stop, and all the old feelings rushed back. Here we go again: no work, no income, how are we going to make it through this time? I knew my husband would have felt the same way. We had always known that the contract couldn't last forever, as it wasn't like a permanent job, but deep down we'd hoped and prayed for delays that the day wouldn't come.

This is the time that I started having to try and make plans again, because I knew when my husband stopped working this time around, we would not make it. This time there were no savings or anything to fall back on. I knew that this time we would lose everything; we would not have a home for our family.

It was that same dark hole we'd felt we'd been in before. We had just been getting to a point where we could see a little light, that we'd just hit a slippery part, and yet, here we were falling back to the bottom, and again the little light we'd seen before was gone. I started thinking that I would have to send my mother to live with my aunt. I knew that my aunt and uncle were also going through hard times, as they already had their own older children living with them, but I just felt that at least my mother would have a roof over her head, and she would be with family.

I then had to think of my children. They would have to go and live with my sister, who was living far away at the time. Or I would have to send them to live with their cousins, who were also not really in a good situation. But this way I could ensure that everyone would at least have a roof over their heads and would not be living on the streets.

I still had my permanent job, so I knew that I could buy extra food for my mother and my children or send money to who they were living with. This was my biggest fear: that we would all end up on the streets. I had to think of ways to ensure that everyone would have a roof over their heads. My husband was not happy with my idea of splitting the family up, and he was not happy that I was even thinking of these things, but I was just trying to make plans for the worst and for what I thought would happen.

Then one day driving along a road, I saw a caravan park not too far from my daughter's school. It gave me an idea. I couldn't let my daughter not go to school. She had to; this was important. It was her future we were talking about. She needed to learn. (At this point, my son was still young enough that he didn't need to go to school.) I drove past slowly again. There was an open spot in the caravan park that I could see from the road, a spot where I thought we could live in my car. We also had a small two-man tent, so perhaps we could stay there when we lost our house. Maybe the children could sleep in the car, and my husband and I could sleep in the tent. This meant we would all be together.

When I told my husband about this idea, he got very upset with me. I knew he felt like he was failing us, that he felt just like me—and possibly worse with the situation we were in—but I told him I would rather plan for the worst than wait for it to happen, and then have all the stress and worries of trying to make plans at the last minute. This way I could work things out and see what would be the best. He said that I shouldn't worry, that things would be okay and that it would work out. At that moment he still had his contract and was working, and he was already finding out about other contracts and jobs coming up. I then thought it best not to keep telling him of my plans or ideas, as this was upsetting him even more. I knew, just like me, he felt like he had the world on his shoulders, and his legs were buckling. But no matter what, we would not give up trying; we just had different ways of dealing with the stress and worries.

I knew from that moment that I now had no one I could talk to about our situation, about how I was feeling and how to work through things. I knew I had to just keep everything to myself. I went back to trying to be positive, acting like there was nothing wrong, that everything was going to be fine. But deep down, the pain, fear, and worry were growing, and I couldn't show this to anyone any more.

Every day when I woke up, I could see no light at the end of the tunnel, and yes, my faith was falling apart. And no matter how hard I tried, I just found myself asking why.

Why God are you doing this? Why? What have we done that is so terrible? There are people out there who do worse things than us. Why is this happening to us? Why are we being punished so badly? Why? Why?

Then my husband got news that his contract would be ending the following month. At that point all the feelings came rushing back again: disappointment, sadness, heartbreak, worry, fear and feeling dead on the inside. The walls of the deep dark hole were now closing in, and somehow, when we thought we had hit the bottom, here we were still sinking in the mud, and there was nothing we could do. I knew my husband would be feeling the same. He had already started looking for work when the rumours first started that the contract was coming to an end, but things in South Africa were still bad and there were no job opportunities for him.

Thinking of the End

One afternoon after work, I think I may have hit my lowest point ever. I was alone in my car and stuck in traffic but thought that maybe, just maybe, if I killed myself, my family could then get the money from the life policy I had. This was an idea I thought could work. But I would have to make sure that they could not say that I'd committed suicide, because if they knew this, the policy would not pay out. I started thinking about how to do it and where. I drove over a bridge each day, so I thought this was a place where I could make it look like an accident if I drove off. Or I could just swerve and drive into a concrete wall on the highway.

Every day going to work and driving home I was looking at my options, and thinking of the timing. I didn't want anyone else to get hurt in my accident, so my timing would have to be perfect, as the roads were always busy, and I couldn't contemplate the idea that I might hurt, or even worse kill someone else.

I kept having this thought in the back of my mind: what happens if I end up not killing myself but just hurting myself badly, to the point where I couldn't work anymore, meaning more costs for my family, more pain and worries. We would end up in an even worse situation than we were in now.

I also started thinking about leaving my family behind if I went through with my plan: the pain and sadness they would have to go through. Yes, they might have some money to live off, but the cost of the funeral would take money away, and how long would it take for them to pay the money out, and how much would they actually get after all deductions and hidden costs? Would it actually be in time to help my family, and would it be enough? I just had this feeling deep inside that taking my own life was not the way out. It might not help my family the way I thought it would. I had to find another way.

At this stage I felt empty inside, like I had no feelings inside me, no sadness, anger, nothing. I felt empty. However when I had to speak, I would have to hold back the tears, because all I wanted to do was break down and cry. And when people looked at me, again all I wanted to do was cry. It was odd, as I had no feelings inside.

Then one morning I arrived at work feeling like a zombie. I knew that come the end of the month, we would not be able to afford to pay for our house, meaning that all the fears and plans of being homeless were going to come true in a few days, and there was nothing I could do to stop or fix it.

I kept myself to myself every day, trying not to talk to anyone in the office. However, sitting there, looking and hearing people discuss things like going on holiday, shopping, complaining, and normal office chit-chat got to me.

I just had to get up and out as soon as possible, as I could feel my tears were coming.

In that next moment, before I got up, it felt as if I was in a film; I saw myself quiet in a corner behind my computer, trying to act like I was working, the people around me were talking and laughing, like nothing was wrong while I knew that in a few days everything was going to fall apart for my family and me, and there was nothing I could do about it. After this scene in my head, I had to get up and get out, so I went out to the company car park. I had to pull myself together, look at something else, and get away from people so that I didn't break down in front of everyone in the office.

After a while, when I came back into the office, the air felt thick. I found it hard to breathe. Our receptionist said that the company director wanted to see me in his office. In that split second all the feelings came rushing to me again; the tears were almost there again. I wondered what had I done now? Had I made a mistake, because to be honest I couldn't tell you what I'd worked on at work over the past few months. I had to try hard not to show my emotions.

I walked down to his office, trying again to pull myself together. I walked in, and he told me to close the door. This was always a bad sign, as the door would only be closed if it was a serious discussion. In those few seconds that it took for me to walk and close the door, I wondered what else was going to happen? Had I made a huge mistake? Was I going to lose my job? What? What else. Please, Jesus, I can't take much more bad news.

As I turned to walk back to his desk to sit down, I couldn't even think of what, or whose policies I had worked on over the past few days, weeks or even months, and as I sat down, I just looked at him, ready to be told more bad news, or receive a warning, or be told I'd made a costly mistake and I was sacked.

He looked at me, sat back in his chair and then asked me what was going on. Just that one question. In that next second, which felt like a lifetime, everything that I had bottled up, all my feelings, thoughts, tears, everything came rushing back like a huge wave: the burning feeling in your chest, the shaking that comes when you try and keep everything back, when you feel you can't breathe anymore. I wanted to burst out crying because I knew that I couldn't do anything else, but at the same time I felt like I couldn't say a word, I couldn't get out of this situation. I couldn't get up and walk out, or run away. I had to try keep it together and simply answer the question.

That was it. Here was the start of not being able to keep it all back. My eyes were burning, and they started to fill with tears, but that first tear couldn't come. I looked around, up and down, to try and stop it, but I couldn't. I looked at him, and as that tear rolled down, I said in a shaking voice, still trying hard to keep it all back, that I was just going through a hard time and didn't really want to talk about it. I wanted to get up. I needed to go. So I said that I just needed to get back to work. But as I got up, he said, 'Please, you need to sit down.'

I looked at him and couldn't hold it back any more. The tears started streaming down my face. *No more hiding or trying to keep it back now*, I thought. I looked at him through the tears and said that he didn't need to worry about me; I was just working through some things like everyone else.

He then told me to sit down again. And while the tears were rolling down, it became a different type of crying. I wasn't doing the sort of crying when your nose runs and you can't talk, it was simply tears running down. He said, 'You need to tell me what is going on.' And trying not to tell him too much about the hard times we had been through, and were still going through, and how things just seemed to get worse every day, I told him about that we were going through a difficult period, and that things with my husband's work situation and our finances were not good.

Just talking briefly about things, I realised that the tears had stopped. We talked about how when we have slipped down the slippery slope and we are in a dark hole, that once we get to the bottom there is only one way left, and that is to start the climb up again.

He then asked me again what else was going on. He said there was something else, more specific, not just general hard times. He said if he could help, he would. But I would need to be honest with him and tell him what the real problem was. So then I told him that due to our financial situation we would not be able to make the payment on our house and a few other bills that we had fallen behind on, and it was hard to make plans when there were no other options, as all other routes had been exhausted.

It was hard sharing this with someone, especially the company director of the situation—even if it was an outline of the situation—but it was now said and done.

He then looked around and said, 'If I can help you out this month with some extra money, will you be okay for the months to follow?' In that moment I said yes, even though I knew that it might not be true. So he asked me to tell him the amounts, which I did. I didn't know at that moment why this happened to me, but after that we spoke a while about faith and how important it is, and that we should never lose faith no matter how hard things are. (He, too, was a Christian and also going through his own hard times with sickness.)

I thanked him for the talk, and in that moment, I felt relief. When I got up to leave the office, I thought while walking back to my desk that this was a miracle from God. He'd heard my prayer for help, and while this was only a month's help, it was a good feeling. I could breathe just that little easier and that dead weight I was carrying seemed to lift just slightly.

Things Need to Get Better

My husband was still looking for work and he was sending out his CV every day, to all sorts of different places, for different types of jobs, as any income would be better than none. We kept praying, but I must admit that my husband and I both wondered why we were being punished, and why was Jesus doing this to us. We just didn't understand. We'd always tried to do things right, but life just seemed to keep getting worse. We knew that by the end of the following month we would have to make drastic changes, as we were now way over our heads in debit.

Out of our costs my husband's car was just about the same amount a month as our house, and we knew that we would have to make the hardest choice; we would have to hand my husband's car back to the bank, as we could not carry both high costs any more, and it was more important to have a roof over our heads. And we still had my car.

This was a hard time for my husband. He had worked so hard to finally get the car of his dreams, and now he was going to lose it, but not on his own terms, and it was hard for him to admit that there was no other choice. I know it might seem odd saying that it was hard to hand back a car, but there was more to this. It meant that all our fears were slowly coming true. We were on the road to losing everything we had, and this was the first of our big things we were losing.

My husband then made the tough call to the bank, informing them that he could no longer pay for the car, even on the lower payments that had been arranged. And as we were already behind on payments, they agreed and came to collect it a few days later.

All men who love cars will understand how difficult this was for my husband. He had worked so hard all his life to have the car he loved, and now he had to stand back and see it taken away, knowing there was nothing he could do because he could no longer afford it. We knew that things were falling apart quickly, and that there were still more hard times ahead, and hard choices to be made. Not easy for a man, I don't think, to see everything slip away.

Here we were again for the next two months: stressed, not knowing how much longer we could keep doing this to survive. But somehow Jesus provided for us and helped us get through. Yes, we had to sell a lot of other things, like bicycles, my daughter's little motorbike that she'd had, and a lot of other small things, just to make it through the month.

The everyday stress and worries were now so normal that once again I was going through the everyday motions like a zombie, worrying about food, what we were going to do day in and day out, and how we were going to make it through. I could see everything coming to an end more now than ever. We would be homeless and starving soon, as my little salary was not enough to keep us going on this road. Somewhere, something had to change, and soon.

Then a miracle happened. My husband's one friend knew of a company that was looking for a temporary employee, as they had too much work. The job didn't pay very much, but something was better than nothing, and this could just keep us going until my husband found a better job.

So my husband started working for this company, and while the costs and worries didn't stop, we were just able to keep our heads above the water. The everyday costs of living kept going up and I had to keep looking at how to cut costs where I could. I also had to sell my car, as it was a Clio and too small for us as a family of five (my mother was also still living with us). I only had a year left to pay off, but I had to get a bigger car for us that would cost less per month. My husband was able to find one that would work out to be cheaper, so we exchanged my car. Things were beginning to settle down for now. It was still not easy, but we could just manage to scrape through each month.

Throughout our challenges we still had my husband's younger sister asking for money and needing help. My sister was also not doing very well either. It seemed that she, too, was going through some hard times. She'd had an offer of work far away from where we stayed and she thought it would be the best option she had, so she was going to take it.

A few months passed and things were sort of staying stable—still hard but okay. My husband's job was fine, but he had to travel to different places, which caused a few problems, as we only had one car now. But we found ways around it.

Then my sister called me one day to say she was not doing well where she was living and working. She was extremely unhappy and she had decided that she would be leaving our country and going back to the UK. However, she couldn't just leave, as she had to sort out a few details.

I then told her that we were not in a great financial position, but if she needed a place to stay, she was welcome to come and live with us until she left. I could just tell in her voice that she needed urgently to get out of the place she was in.

About a month later my sister arrived, and it was a blessing in disguise at the time. She had a car. The fact that my husband had to travel for his job was making it harder for me to get to work and to get my daughter to and from school. But as my sister was here now, she could help with the travelling up and down.

While my husband was working for his current company, he was advised that his previous company, which had originally made him redundant, was looking for people again. It would not be on a permanent basis but rather on a fixed-term contract. We had to consider this option carefully, as the current job would also come to an end, as it was just temporary, and we couldn't bear to go through another period of unemployment.

Just as we received this news about his old company, the director of my husband's current employment said that the work he'd employed my husband for was coming to an end. This man had helped us a lot in the short time my husband had worked for him. If we'd needed money for petrol or something, he had understood and paid a small amount of my husband's salary in advance. He also agreed that he would try his best to keep my husband working while we waited to hear if my husband could get a contract back with his old company.

Within the next few weeks my husband did get a contract back with his old company and returned to the place that had made him redundant.

My husband and I were happier that he would be back in a company that paid better. However, we still had to get through the first month, and the travelling costs were going to be a challenge, as he was working in the office and this was on the opposite side of the city we lived in. We knew it would be a challenge, but we knew that we could manage somehow.

My husband's first project back was to be out in a country called Botswana. The company applied for a temporary work visa for him and he had to travel by car to get to the site. Our problem was that we had no money to pay for his travel costs up front. (The company would only reimburse him at the end of the month.) But we had no choice. He would have to go and I was going to try and find a way to get money to him to pay for his travel down.

Everything I tried to get extra money was not working. Items I tried to sell had no value and I was having a difficult time scraping money together for my husband. But I just kept trying and selling what we had left to make some money to give him.

At this time my sister was still living with us while she was preparing to leave for the UK the following month. I knew she also didn't have much money, but at the same time I knew that she had money saved to help her survive when she went over to the UK. I didn't have a choice. I had to ask my sister if I could borrow money from her—just to help my husband get to his place of work. I promised her that I would pay her back before she left at the end of the month, and thankfully she agreed, but I could see she was not happy about it. While I understood that she didn't have a lot, and I understood she would need the money herself once she'd left, I knew that I would be giving it back to her, so at the same time I didn't understand why she felt or looked reluctant to help us.

I felt a little down about this. She had been staying with us for a few months now, and she hadn't taken out any of her money while she was with us. She only took out her own money when it was something she did on her own or something she wanted for herself. Moreover, the amount I borrowed was not much, so it was a little hard for me to get over her attitude of not really wanting to help us.

I understood that she was also under a lot of pressure and was worried about when she got to the UK, about what she was going to do. But she had family and friends in the UK who were going to help her, and she already had a place to stay there. And everyone there was willing to help her get set up and started. I know it's not easy to rely on other people and accept help, but at least she had people willing to help her.

Then later that day I encountered another problem: I couldn't transfer the money to my husband while he was travelling. The bank machines were not working. I didn't know what to do, but once again Jesus helped us. When my husband reached the border, he could finally find a bank machine and withdraw some money, and he made it to his place of work.

Days passed and the month was coming to an end. My sister was getting ready to leave. I think she was happy and excited but worried all at the same time. However, as soon as I got my salary, I paid her back the money she had lent us. She left for the UK a few days later.

Things Started to Get Better

While we were happy that my husband had a well-paid job again, and things were starting to look better, it didn't help much at that stage because we were so far behind on bills that our situation didn't improve quickly. It was going to take us a while to get back on top of things. The good news was that we were now actually making it up the steep slippery sides of the big black hole that we were in, and we could see a much bigger light coming down on us.

After a few months my sister told me that we should contact the UK immigration, as they had changed the laws, which could make it possible for me to get a British passport. I didn't really want to get my hopes up again, as we'd looked at this before, so I thanked her for the news and put off looking into it. We had tried so hard before to look at ways to leave South Africa, and they had all failed miserably, and I also thought that Jesus didn't want us to leave our country. We were just getting on a better road again with our life, and I didn't really want to go off the path now and cause more issues for ourselves.

However, after a few months, as things in our country were not getting any better, my husband had a better paid job, and things were improving with our situation, I had a feeling that maybe we should find out if I could get a UK passport. I didn't think it could hurt to investigate.

My husband's job was on a month-to-month rolling contract, so it meant that at any time it could end. This was not really a nice feeling to have, living month to month, never knowing if this was the last month he had work. If it did come to an end, we knew that we would be back to losing everything again. It was a horrible feeling never knowing what was going to happen, and it was so stressful as we couldn't plan anything. All we wanted was stability.

At this time, I experienced a strange feeling that the journal my sister in-law had given me a while ago that was lying in the back of my cupboard. Had to be used to write down everything that we had been through in the last few years and all that we were going though in our lives at the time. Then I wondered if I was just being silly. I didn't need to write it all down; this was more for teenagers writing about everyday things. But no matter how hard I tried to ignore this feeling, it just kept popping back in my head. Over and over my mind would drift and then I felt I had to write. I had to write, and I needed to write, now!

I thought that maybe writing would be a good way to express how I was feeling, as I didn't have anyone who I could speak to about things that worried me, or how I felt about things. So I started the journal by making a list of what I really wanted in our lives at that time, which was for my daughter to do well at school, to have my psoriasis and arthritis gone, and for my husband to get a permanent well-paid job so that he could be home with us every day instead of working away for long periods.

I decided then it was time to investigate whether I could get my UK passport, so I logged on and read all the details online. As I was reading through, I got excited, as did my husband, because now it seemed I did stand a good chance of being eligible to obtain a UK passport. This felt like a door being opened for us again to possibly leave our country. I completed all the forms and sent off all the details and documents they requested.

After about two months I had a reply from the immigration office to say that they needed more details and documents, and I had a timeline to get everything back to them. The problem was that everything had to be an original, so it all took time, as everything had to be posted to London.

We had most of the documents, except for my vault birth certificate. If you don't know what this is (as I didn't know at the time), it is the certificate that was handwritten at the time I was born. When we made an enquiry to request this document from the Home Office, they responded by saying that it could take months before I could get a copy of it, as this document is kept in some huge archive vault. *Great*, I thought. *So close. Once again the door has been slammed shut in our faces.* It just felt that every time we tried to leave the country or thought that there was a door opened for us, something would happen and stop us. And here we were again.

My husband and I felt down and disappointed, and just didn't know what to do. I didn't have months to provide the one document, however, I thought what I could do was write to them and explain that we would have to wait for the certificate. They then replied and gave an extension for an additional month from the original due date. However, they said that they could not extend it any further than that. I was so happy, as this meant that we had extra time to try and get this one document. All I could do was pray that it could be found in the following few weeks.

I prayed and asked Jesus to help us. If this was what God wanted for us, if this was the door that God had opened for us to leave the country, then I would ask, 'Please, Lord, I need your help again', as there was nothing I could do from my side. I was now relying on other people to find one sheet of paper in what sounded like a needle in a haystack.

We really thought that God wanted us to leave, as we'd had this feeling for years that we had to leave our country. But originally, I hadn't qualified for a UK passport before then, with the Australian route that didn't work out, and then my husband losing his job, and us almost losing everything. I thought I was wrong again about this feeling, and that it was just me wanting to leave.

I couldn't believe that everything was now hanging and it all came down to this one paper, which could stop us from finding out if I could get a UK passport, so deep down I guess I was wrong again: that we were not meant to leave.

My husband's brother-in-law was also in the process of working to get his ancestry visa sorted for the UK. In talking they discussed a company that could obtain documents in a week when it would normally take months. But they charged a high fee. We took the details and decided that we should just pay the fee and get the certificate sooner.

I then wondered again, was this Jesus answering my prayer for help? Did we get this number so that I could obtain the certificate in time? I thought it was. We therefore completed some forms and paid the fees—by this time we didn't have much longer to get the document back—and sent it off to the UK.

A few days later the person at the company called us to say that they were having a problem locating my certificate, that they would keep trying to push, but he couldn't guarantee that I would have my certificate soon. Here we are again, just when we think things are working for us and not against us, something else happens and seems to close the door in our faces again. This was really getting annoying and hard to deal with and making it even harder to keep positive.

In general, our lives and situation were better and life was improving, but at the same time, it was no fun or less worrying when you live month to month, not knowing when everything might come tumbling down again. There were no other permanent jobs out there for my husband. Everything was contract-based, so moving to another company would not help us. With his current company at least he knew the people, and the work he was doing, and that if things were going to change, he would know in advance.

I then thought that while it was not easy or a wonderful feeling to have this continuous disappointment when we tried to find a way to leave our country, I had to remember the positives: my husband had a job now, he was earning a salary, and we were living a sort of normal life, so maybe we were not meant to leave our country in the way I thought. It was hard. But I then tried to be more positive and make everyone else around me more positive, deciding that it was in God's hands. If it was God's plan for us to leave our country, I would get the certificate in time; if it was not what he wanted, then I needed to stop trying so hard to push for us to leave. Because at the end of the day, God knows what is best for us, and while we don't or may never understand, we just need to accept things.

I decided to look at the different visa options for the UK just in case I did get my passport. The best visa option for the children and my husband was called a spousal visa, but one of the requirements was that you had to have a job offer in the UK or be working in the UK for at least 6 months. This was only one of the requirements we had to meet from a very long list.

If we did choose to do the spousal visa, it would not be easy. We would have to pull my daughter out of school and do home schooling, as my husband would have to leave his job so that I could work in the UK for at least 6 months. To do this, my husband and children would have to travel over on visitor visas first so that we could be together while I worked for 6 months. However, the maximum time for a visitor visa is 6 months, so this meant that my children and husband would have to return to our country after that period and we would have to apply for visitor visas again if I was not working long enough. The worst thing was that we could only apply for the spousal visa from outside of the UK, meaning that when we were ready to apply, the children and my husband would have to return to South Africa and we would be apart until a decision was made. And this could take months.

I kept looking more into the visa options. One of the other requirements was that you had to earn a certain amount per year to qualify. This worried me, as my salary at the time was not enough. However, on further reading, I saw that they might look at both my salary and my husband's. This made me feel better, as the minimum salary limit required was high if you were not earning pounds, and our country's currency was not very good.

I know you may think it was silly of me looking at all the visa options and requirements, if I didn't even have my certificate that they wanted, and we didn't even know if I would get my British passport, but I'm one of those people who needs to know what we would be in for in order to be prepared for what might come, and what was required.

Let the Years Roll On

As we were just waiting for my certificate, with things looking better and our lives settling down, another blow came. We were now in September and my husband had his contract renewal again. This was only until the end of November. Before it had never really stated an end date, but this time it did. In that next second all I could think was, *Really, Jesus, WHY? Why does this keep happening?* Everything was on hold again. The stress and worries were back in an instant. We couldn't afford to go through a bad patch again; I knew that we would not survive this time. I prayed to God to please not let my husband lose his job again. I had to place this in God's hands because I knew I couldn't handle the stress, disappointment and hurt on my own again.

I don't know how to explain this feeling, but I'm sure many of you know, yes, we all have the everyday stress and worries, but when bad things happen over and over again, you build up an anxiety and fear to bad news. You know it might come but you try to ignore things, and when it does come, all the old feelings rush back. In that instant you feel nothing and everything at the same time: pain, anger, hurt, disappointment, and the heart-wrenching sadness that brings you to your knees, as it takes away all your strength and you can't breathe.

Please, Lord, please, Jesus, I can't do this again!

Two days later my husband came home and told me that one of the managers on the project had told him not to worry; he would be kept on the project until March the following year, as there was still a lot of work to be done. *Thank you, God, for answering my prayers.* And in that moment again the relief was fantastic. I felt like I could breathe again, the worry and stress lifted and I felt as if the world had lifted from my shoulders.

In October I finally got a reply that my vault birth certificate was on its way. I was so happy but worried as the deadline for sending it to the UK was extremely close now. Then with about 3 days before the due date, I received a letter in the post. It was the certificate. I immediately sent an email to the UK Home Office to say that I was posting the document as requested. I sent off the certificate and prayed to Jesus that they would accept all the details we'd provided, and that I would get my British passport. If I didn't, then that was it: I would accept that God didn't want us to leave our country.

I was also trying hard to get my religious life right with Jesus, to try to see where my faults were. The one thing

I realised was, that when I speak about things with people, I don't mention Jesus or God, and what he has done in our lives. I knew that was something I needed to start working on. In saying this, it was also hard because some people just don't seem to hear if you do refer to Jesus, and others seem offended by it, and switch off. Because of this it was hard to read a situation and a person to know what and when the right time was to refer to Jesus in a conversation. I didn't want to become like one of those people who preach to every person, or to put people off, making them want to avoid me or speaking with me. That was not what I wanted, and I would not be able to spread God's word in this way.

The British Home Office had been in contact and was still looking at my passport application. As my mother had been married three times, I would have to provide documents to show her surname changes over the years. Luckily, my mother had kept all her documents, so we had all the marriage certificates and divorce certificates. Again, I had to post all the documents over. Every time I did this, I had to pay to track the envelope to ensure it was delivered within 2 days to the UK Home Office. I had to pray to Jesus that they would accept this as proof of my mother's surname changes.

About a week later I had an email from the UK; they wanted additional documents for my mother's first marriage. (This was the marriage where she obtained her British citizenship.) On reading what they wanted, I just panicked, I had been praying so hard that there would be no problems, and that everything would be accepted, but now they had requested documents that we didn't have. We are talking about documents that would have been over 60 years old, and I had no idea if we could find them. And I wouldn't even know where to start looking, or who to approach, and yes, while my mother kept most her documents, these documents we didn't have. In that moment I thought this was it; God didn't want us to leave. He'd brought us this far only to let everything fall apart. Then I thought, *No, it's not the end. I just need to pray and ask God: Is this the end of this road? What do I need to do?* There was no quick reply (which I think so many of us wish and hope for).

A few days later I had a thought: what if my mother provided an affidavit? This is a written statement, signed under oath, to say that the details provided in your statement are true. I sent an email to the UK to ask if they would accept this, as we didn't have the documents they wanted. Again, all I could do was pray and try to believe that this would succeed.

The following day, they replied and confirmed that they would accept this from my mother. *Thank you, Jesus, you have answered my prayers again.* I felt relieved again. We arranged to have the affidavit done, and my mother confirmed all the details they wanted. I sent this off, and we had to wait again.

After about a week I went online to track details of the application, but there was nothing. All I could see was that all documents were being reviewed.

After a while longer had passed and there was no change to the update, I sent them an email to follow up. They replied simply to confirm that the application was been looked at.

As I didn't hear anything and there were no updates, the same feeling came back. I must be wrong; God didn't want us to leave. I decided to forget about leaving our country, and the application, and we just carried on with our lives.

After a while I received a letter from the UK containing some of the original documents we had submitted. There were no other details, just a note to say they had returned all the documents. I logged in to the website again to see if there was any update online, but there was still no change. When I tried to follow up with an email, they just said that they were not able to assist me, as they were not authorised to give me the details. Why would they send back my documents, not provide any update, and not want to tell me what was going on? All I wanted to know was, yes, it was successful or sorry, it was rejected. However, all they said was that the outcome would be sent to me by post once completed. This gave us hope that I would get my British passport. We just had to be patient. Patience is one of the hardest things for me. I wanted an answer now. I wanted to know what was happening now. But there was nothing I could do but wait.

About two weeks after that, my sister-in-law and mother-in-law were coming over to visit. We were going to have a *braai*, or as most of you may know it, a barbeque, just to have a nice family day, as they were also still going through some hard times. But I think God had a bigger plan.

At the last minute we realised we needed some extra food. My husband had to quickly jump in the car and find a shop to buy it, as it was a public holiday and not many places were open. My husband and my mother had just left the house when my husband's mother and sister arrived. When they walked in, something felt different. My sister-in-law had three sons, on this occasion, they were not with her. They were with their father for the day. I had this feeling that I had to give them a message, a message that faith is all we need, no matter what we are going through. But how could I just tell them this, I wondered, so we just had a casual, normal chat about how everyone was.

Somehow we got onto the subject of faith and God. I can remember them sitting around our outside table and I was standing. I'd started trembling. I didn't know why, but I told them what was lying ahead of us with the visas if I got my passport and we moved to the UK. I also explained that we would need over a million rand in our bank account just to get approved for the visas. We didn't have this kind of money—this was the kind of money only rich people had—and we didn't even know how we would get it.

I then explained all that had been happening to us over the past few years: when my husband had lost his job, when we'd had no money, and when we'd come so close to losing everything. During these times God had been with us and helped us, even when we hadn't realised it. He'd provided us with food every day. And I know what I'm about to say will sound impossible, but I told them that I would only have a little bit of money left at the end of the month in the hard times, and somehow I used money, but the money seemed to always be there when I needed it. I don't mean huge amounts, I just mean that somehow, I would withdraw money to buy food for a few days, knowing I almost had nothing left. Then knowing we would need food again, I would withdraw money again and notice I had a little more than I expected in the bank. So when I thought I could only buy food for a day, I could buy food for a few days again.

Yes, we had to sell a lot of our things and it didn't happen all the time, but when I think back on it now, I have no idea how we made it through the months during the period when we had nothing. It could only have been Jesus helping us. He had provided just enough to get us through, even though at the time it didn't feel as if He was with us or helping us, I could see now that he was.

The hard times were very hard, and at the time I didn't know how or if we were going to make it through, but there we were still standing, and I knew that God would be there and help us going forward no matter what came our way. We just had to keep believing, have faith that this was God's plan. When it is his plan, there is nothing that God can't do, no matter how hard it is at times for us. We spoke about Jesus, faith, problems and hard times for over an hour, and just as we finished, my husband arrived home, God's timing is perfect! I just hope that I gave them the message that God wanted them to hear, and that I lifted them up to see that there is a light at the end of the tunnel.

Later in the day I was in the kitchen and my husband's mother came to me. She thanked me for the talk, and she said that hearing and seeing my faith had made her feel so much better. In that moment as she walked away, I said, 'Thank you, Jesus. Thank you for giving me the opportunity to tell others about how God helped us, how faith was hard but important. '

Faith helps with hope if we lose hope. Well, let's just say, as we all know in one way or another if we lose hope, everything else seems worthless and we fall into a very deep, dark hole.

Changes

I realised my stress levels were high, and the worries ever growing, so I decided then that I had to try and change. I knew that I was quick to anger and I was taking my frustration and stress out on my family, I was not a very nice person to be around, and deep down I knew that this was not what God wanted, so I slowly tried to concentrate on my outbursts and bring myself into a happier place.

A few days later I received a message to say that a DHL package was on its way to be delivered. I didn't know what it was but then remembered that the UK used DHL. I was hoping that it would be my new British passport— or the letter saying that the application was unsuccessful. When the package was delivered by DHL, my mother phoned me at work to say that it was from the UK, I asked her to open it to see what it was. She did, but then she paused and said that it was simply all of the remaining documents we had sent through for the application. I was now worried. Why did it only have the last documents we sent? What was the outcome? There was no letter or any details to say what had happened. So I sent an email to the last person I'd dealt with at the UK immigration office. She replied the following day, saying that she could see the application had been completed, and that a passport had been issued. In that moment of reading the email I just felt, *WWWHHHHAATTT! God has made it possible for me to get my UK passport, he has opened the door for my family and me, so this means that the feeling that we must or will leave our country was right.*

On the 9th of November 2018 I got home and there in the post was my British passport. How great is our God! Looking at the passport details there were no funny restrictions. I was now noted as a British citizen. The following day on my way to work, I was overwhelmed with happiness. I was excited and felt hopeful. I had not felt real happiness for some time, and it just felt wonderful to be happy.

The short period of happiness faded slightly as I then started thinking of how on earth we were going to get to the UK and meet all the requirements—and find the large amounts of money we needed. I knew this was just the next step and that we would have to pray and ask God to show us where and what we needed to do to make this happen.

Very quickly the happiness was gone and the worries and impossibilities came flooding in. The options we had would mean that I would have to leave my family for 6 months or more, and we would need large amounts of money, money that only the really rich have. And here we were with not much to our names, looking at these requirements and thinking, *How will we do this? It is impossible!*

As I was working, I couldn't let anyone know what we were considering doing, so I had to ask my mother to call the visa agency and see if they could provide us with details about the process of the visas and what other options there might be for us which would not require me to leave my family or demonstrate we had the large amount of money they seemed to require us to have.

Unfortunately, my hopes came crashing down after my mother had spoken to the agency. I had thought that as I'd obtained my citizenship through my mother, that we could do the same for my children—almost like an ancestry visa. Unfortunately, that is not how the UK works.

Here we go again, another mountain, another climb that seems impossible, more worries and sadness to get through. I knew that all I could do was pray to Jesus and ask for guidance. If this was what he wanted for us, that I was right about the feeling we should leave. He would help make this possible for us. But I will admit I was getting more and more saddened, as I didn't see how we could get this visa after reading more about what we would need, and all the requirements that had to be met. So I contacted the visa agents and asked if they could investigate all the options available to us to obtain visas for my family.

December is when the school year ends in South Africa, and I received my daughter's report. Here was another knock (again)—not only for me but also for my daughter. I had to tell her that she hadn't passed the year, so she couldn't move up to the next year level. She was only eight at the time. We had tried so hard during the year to help; she'd even gone for extra lessons. We'd had so many teachers trying to help her. Even the small changes I'd made by trying to be more positive with her hadn't helped. After leaving it in God's hands and praying to God to help her, it had all been for nothing.

I know, it was not a good time for me and my faith; it was dwindling again. Here I was thinking I was on track with my faith and working hard to ensure I was doing all the right things, that I was understanding what I was feeling, and believing that when we hand it over to Jesus, He will take care of it, but again I was wrong. How is it that I prayed and tried my best, but Jesus didn't hear me, or help as I wanted? I know we can't always get what we want, when we want, but why was my daughter being punished? I thought. I then thought that maybe God was punishing me by letting my daughter fail at school because my faith was not strong enough, and I'd had doubts.

I was upset and hurt, and I had to try explaining to my daughter that when she returned to school the following year, unfortunately, all her friends would be in a year above her. When I told her, her little face broke my heart. I could see she didn't really understand what I was saying, but you could see that she knew it was not a good thing.

I knew that when she went back to school, when she saw that all her friends were in a different year, and class and the younger children were now in her class with her. she would realise what I had been trying to explain. And I knew it would be hard for her.

I thought to myself that I needed to pull myself together, for my daughter, to help and support her even more, and that maybe it was better this had happened now rather than later in her life, as children can be cruel to each other.

That following day the visa agents came back to me and confirmed that the only route we could take was the spousal visa route, the one whereby we needed the large amount of money and had to meet all the other requirements. Another knock, another disappointment, and another knock on my faith. What did God want from me? Did I get it all wrong? Was it just my wanting to leave the country so badly that I'd made myself think this was what God wanted. Was I jealous of other people? That they had everything easy, and that all would go well for them, and everything just fell into place for them, no matter whether they believed in God or not. Maybe it was all my fault, that I'd been putting myself and my family through hard times, and for what? Nothing?

I was angry with myself. However, a few days later I realised that I was being stupid. I know how great God is. He'd helped us get through really hard times already, and he had made it possible for me to get my British passport. And yes, it all seemed impossible and we'd had bad news, but all things are possible through God. I just had to remember that, no matter how difficult it was. I had to believe that God would not open the door for me to get my British passport only to close that same door in our faces.

A short while later I received a text message from a friend. It had a gloomy picture attached of a small old bridge that disappeared up into the fog. The bridge looked half broken and impossible to walk on, and at the bottom it said: Faith is trusting God even when you don't understand his plan. I felt that this was an answer to all my uncertainty and frustration, that I just had to keep working on my faith and trusting God.

Keeping the Faith

My husband was contacted by an old colleague about a possible well-paid job that was coming up in Iraq. Not one of the best places to work, I know, but his salary would be excellent. If he did take this job, it would give us the finances that we needed for the visas so that we could apply from our country and I wouldn't have to leave my family for 6 months. It would take all that stress of meeting the financial requirements away. However, as quickly as the possible job offer came, so it went, so I had to go back to trying to calculate how we could make things work.

If we didn't have the huge amount of money as savings, I either needed a job offer from the UK, or I had to be working in the UK for 6 months before we could make the application. I also needed a specific minimal annual salary. The only way to do this was to apply for work from our home country, or go over to the UK and find a job. No company was going to hire me if I was not in the UK, I knew this, as I work in the insurance industry. It's not a job that normally recruits internationally. Therefore, the only option, we had was for me to go to the UK and find work that would meet the requirements for the visa. But I had this huge sadness in my heart. I couldn't leave my family behind for 6 months. I didn't want to do this. Just thinking of leaving our children for a day was an issue for me, and now I had to consider leaving them for 6 months, or longer, and I didn't think God would let that happen. The other issue was that even if I got a job and worked for 6 months, when it came to applying for the visas, we would have to do it from South Africa, and this process could take three months or more. No company would give me a 3-month holiday to be with my family while we waited for an outcome.

Now I felt stuck. I didn't know what to do. The only real option we had was to be patient and try our best to save up the large amount of money we needed so that we didn't have to worry about me getting a job in the UK first with the required annual salary. However, at the same time, this was not a nice thought, as saving up this amount of money would take years, and in that time the cost of everything in life, with visas costs, would just keep increasing, meaning that the end of the race would never come, as the finish line would keep moving. At the same time, we were still in the same boat: my husband was on a month-to-month contract with his company, so we were in a bad situation not knowing what the next month would bring.

We were now in December 2018, and heading for the end of the year. I was just looking forward to the New Year and hoping it would be better for us. We had so many bad years and this year was not done yet. Shortly after this, another blow came. They gave my husband another month's contract, but they reduced his salary by 20 per cent. This was a big reduction and would knock us back with our finances again, as we were still trying to sort things from the time when my husband had no work. So that was it, the last straw, the last thing I needed. I think God just confirmed that we were to stay in our country.

I went into a dark place again, questioning God. *Why? Why put us through this? What is it that we do that is so wrong? Why are we being punished? Why must we battle like this all the time? Why can't things come right? What does it help to pray, if he never listens or answers?*

A week later I was stuck in traffic on the highway. Not being able to move I started looking around, and there on one of the buildings was a small electric sign board that flashed up Bible verses. It paused for a while on a sun setting, and I asked God to please speak to me. I asked him to let me know what he wanted from me, or where he wanted us to be, and if he could just tell me what path it was that he wanted us on.

During the day at work, my husband told me that the Iraq job was not totally out the window yet.

When I got home that afternoon after work, my mother's one friend was there visiting. She is a true Christian. I didn't know her that well, but from all the stories that my mother had told me, I knew that she had a good relationship with God. We were talking about general matters and I guess that my mother had mentioned a few things to her about our situations, whereupon her friend told me that I was on the right path and we were going to leave the country. I thought to myself, how odd it was that she had answered exactly the questions I had prayed about earlier that morning.

GOD IS GREAT and amazing. Thank you for answering me, Lord, and letting me know that you are still there, and that we are on the right path, no matter how impossible it looked.

We were now heading for a new year—2019. I prayed that this would be a better year for us.

A New Year

This year started off differently. My husband still had his current work; however, he was contacted for the Iraq job—that had kept popping up and then disappearing—and another company had also contacted him with a job offer. The choices were hard; he could stay with his current company on the month-to-month contract always with the uncertainty of what would happen the following month, not knowing if they would keep cutting his salary, or there was the other job offer, which was based in our country. This meant that he could be home more, as all the other work he had done over the years had always been out the country, away from home for 6 weeks or more at a time. Then there was the Iraq job. This obviously meant working away from home again, in another country, and the time he would be away from home would be up to three months at a time, but the salary for this job was extremely good.

At the same time, we decided that we have to put our faith in Jesus. So we put our house on the market, as we knew that we were on the right path now, and that God would help us reach the goal of leaving our country. We had to remove all doubt, we had to show God that we trusted him completely. Trust me, this was a scary thing for us to do. Here we were putting the house on the market when things were not even clear yet regarding when we would be going, or even if we could go (as we didn't even have the money that we needed for the visas). But we made the decision to place our trust in God fully. We placed everything in his hands, and simply prayed that when the time was right the house would sell.

We were not very clever were we? When I think about it, yes, we wanted to leave the country, we knew we had to have large sums of money to do this (which we didn't have), we had a long list of requirements that had to be met, and we didn't even know if we could meet all of them. And here we were putting even more stress on the situation by trying to sell our house.

At the time we just felt that through the years, through all the hard times, Jesus had always been there and got us through somehow. We believed that He had opened this door for us, and now it was our turn to show God that we trusted Him fully.

As my husband was faced with the two job offers, we were not sure which would be the right one. One offered him more time with us at home with a slightly better salary; the other job meant long times away from us as a family, but the salary was huge and would help with our visa costs more quickly. At the same time we knew it couldn't just be about the money, so I prayed that God would help show my husband what the right choice was.

People were now coming in and making offers on the house. *WHAT NOW? WHAT ARE WE GOING TO DO?* We'd just made this situation harder for ourselves. If we sold the house now, we would have to move, then rent a place until we could get the visas sorted, then we would have to move again. *Man, oh man, this was a HUGE mistake*, I thought. But I had to try and stay calm. We had prayed to God before and said it was all in his hands, so we just had to pray to God again. I asked God that the house would only be sold at the right time, as we didn't want to add more stress and problems to an already uncertain situation.

The devil was trying hard now to break me again, putting doubt and fear in me. I kept thinking, *What on earth are we doing? Why have we put ourselves in this situation? How stupid are we?*

My husband had chosen to accept the Iraq job because it would pay him a high salary over a short period of time. But he would be away from home for over three months.

However, this would open the door for us to complete the visa applications much sooner. This additional income would also help to sort out all our financial issues from the past few rough years. This one job could help wipe our slate clean, then we could start over on a better footing: no debit, no financial worries. Well, that's what we thought at the time anyway.

A lot can happen in a month. Here we were now almost at the end of January. I then made the decision to remove our house from the market. There had been a few offers on it, but up to this point none of the applications had been successful. The stress of what would happen if we sold the house and not being ready to leave the country was getting to me. And it now also looked like the Iraq job offer was not coming through.

At that time, I thought that I had made the right decision by taking the house off the market, as we wouldn't have been able to afford to pack everything up and rent a property while trying to save for the visas. I thought it better that we kept paying off the mortgage on our own house while trying to save for the visas. However, just as all the details were confirmed with the house agents that everything had been cancelled, my husband told me that he had just received his contract for the Iraq job. We agreed not to put the house back on the market until we knew more about when we could leave.

We were both happy that the job had finally come through. It meant that we could now start the process of saving the money we would need for the visas. We both thanked God for answering our prayers again and helping to lead us in the right direction.

FEBRUARY 2019

This month seems to have started off well, but we have had some bad news again. Seems like when something good happens, then straight after this it is followed by something bad.

I know that God is there but I think the devil or someone is trying really hard to get to me and my family. My husband now required a visa to get into Dubai for his new job, and this was proving difficult. The company he was going to work for didn't offer help with the visa application—all they would do was advise what needed to be done and how. We had to do everything ourselves.

In addition to the Dubai visa issue, my son and mother were now both continuously ill, and my daughter was having problems at school. At that moment it just felt like everything was against us again. I had to try and stay positive and remember that together with Jesus, we would make it through.

Just a few days later, my husband was advised by his company that he was not able to return home on his exact 30 days of notice, as they wanted him to complete the work he was busy with. But we really wanted him home so that we could spend time with him before he had to leave for his new job and be away for 3 months. I was praying hard for everything that was going on at that time, as I knew it could only have been evil trying to cause our faith to drop again, trying to cause fear and worry.

After a few days, my husband was advised by his company that he could return home on the original date that was agreed. This was great news, as this meant we could have some family time together before he had to leave again.

At the end of February my husband was going to start his new job. He was not sure what to expect or how it was going to be. All we could do was pray that Jesus would be with him and help him with whatever might happen out on this new site.

My husband got his Dubai visa, my mother and son seemed to be getting better, and things settled down slightly again. My husband left to start his new job, and on his travels there he was advised by different people that Iraqi border people were known to give people a hard time. This stressed my husband and me out. So, while he was waiting, all we could do was pray and pray—as he sat there in the queues —that Jesus would be there and that God would send his angels down to help my husband with whatever may come. When it got to his turn, he had no problems at all, and he went through easily.

Once again, how great is our God! Thank you, Jesus, for being there for us. Thank you for helping my husband.

When my husband arrived on the site, he was advised that he had only 6 days to learn what would be required of him in the new position. This made my husband worry and get stressed, as it turned out that the work was nothing like he'd expected. You see, it was a friend who had told him about the job and recommended him for the position, and this friend had told him that he would be able to do the job, as it was similar to work he'd done before. (We were guessing this is exactly what the friend had told his boss in order to get my husband the job.)

I prayed for my husband. I prayed that God would be with him, help him to learn and help him to remember everything. I know that God had helped us so much already, but I know that we can do all things with Jesus, even if it is hard and looks impossible.

MARCH 2019

Today we made the decision to start our British visa application journey. The first fees have been paid to the immigration agents to start looking into our case and then they will let us know what all the actual requirements are.

A few days later I received the list, hoping that what I had read on the internet was not all going to be applicable for us, however, there was no such luck. Even more was required, and just like we'd always known, there were a few big issues. I had no idea how we would find ways around them. I would definitely need a job offer from the UK, and I didn't have this at that moment. And I had no idea how to get a job offer. There were many job offers online, but because I was not in the UK, this was a problem for most of the companies. Then there was also the uncertainty surrounding when I would actually be in the UK.

One of the other requirements was that we had to show an address in the UK where we would be staying. Once again, another issue; we couldn't rent a place, as we didn't actually know when we would be going. We couldn't say we were going to stay with family, as you have to give details concerning how many rooms they have. We had been advised that if they didn't have enough rooms then the UK immigration office would not accept this and could decline our visa. We'd been advised that the other option we had was to book a hotel or a Bed & Breakfast. But, hey, who has money to book a place like that for at least 6 months? Not us. We had to try and keep costs down as much as possible and a hotel or a Bed & Breakfast would require a deposit before they would confirm anything in writing.

Even if we wanted to consider booking a hotel or bed & breakfast, they wanted dates. And how could we give dates if we had no idea when and if we would get our visas. And what business would let us book a place for 6 months and then ask if we could change the dates halfway through the process? There was too much uncertainty and no place would help us with this, and if they were to consider it, they wanted a huge deposit. The agents we were working with told us there were ways to do things with accommodation and we just needed to see what would be best for us.

Over and above these worries, my husband was having a really hard time trying to take in everything he had to learn in only a few days, and now he was on his own with no real assistance, not sure of what exactly to do. As this job was nothing like he'd been told, we were both a little upset about the situation and the fact that his friend who'd helped him get the job had not been honest with him. We quickly came to realise that his friend had been desperate to have someone to swap out with so he could have a break. He'd not been honest about everything concerning the job, and had just said things to convince my husband it would be easy, as it was similar to what he'd done before. However the work and situation were totally different to what his friend had said and explained.

I knew this was all the devil's work, making all our situations look impossible and putting doubt and fear and sadness into our days. I prayed to Jesus to please step in and help my husband on site and to please help us with finding a way around all the issues we had with the visa requirements.

A week later and Jesus was helping my husband on site. The people he was working with seemed to be nice to him and were understanding that he was new to the job. He sounded better when I spoke to him today, however, I knew that he still had a long way to go with this job and months to get through before he could take a break. I just knew that this would be an ongoing prayer request to ask Jesus to be with him and help him as much as possible.

Regarding the visa requirements, things were not looking any better. People we knew in the UK who had their own companies were not willing to assist me with a job offer.

They said they didn't want to get involved because they were concerned about what would happen if things didn't work out or if there were problems. I tried to explain that I understood their concerns, that it would not be a permanent situation, I didn't expect to actually work for them, all I needed was a job offer; once we had the visas and we were there, I would immediately start looking for a job. But everyone had some excuse as to how or why they couldn't help me. So much for thinking that having family who have their own companies would be an easy answer to our problems! Here we were stuck. No hope, no job offers and no moving forward until I could get this box ticked.

I was reading my Bible one night and I happened upon a section to do with feeling distant from God, and that I should not stop trusting him. Then, just as I walked out of my room the following day, my mother came to me and said she thought she might have an answer to the job offer situation. There is a family member that we don't know very well who has their own company, and they might be willing to help. My mother said all we needed to do was just give them all the details.

I must add the reason why I also think people were not willing to help me, which was that I had to earn a minimum amount of money per year. I think because of this and the small companies that people had, they did not want to put anything in writing, knowing that if they did, it could cause them issues if I came over and they couldn't actually pay me. (I didn't really expect anyone to actually pay me, I just needed the job offer.) This was a huge issue for most people we spoke to, so I really hoped this family member I didn't even know would be willing to help.

By the end of March we were no further on. No one was willing to help—or couldn't help with a job offer—so I had to ask the agents if there was another way. The answer was yes. But this was the one way we had looked at before where you needed a huge amount in a savings account. You had to have all this money in savings to demonstrate that once you went over to the UK it would be enough for you and your family to survive on for at least 6 months. You can just imagine the amount they wanted you to have. All I can say is that this was not a small amount. So once again we were back with the problem that I needed that job offer. So I just had to keep praying to Jesus to help as I didn't know what else to do.

My husband was also stressed—not only about this visa application, but about a planned shut-down on site. He was worried as he had no idea what to expect and what would be expected of him. Lord, oh Lord, please, we need your help: help with the visas, and help with my husband's job.

It's important to understand something. The company my husband had worked for before was huge and there was a lot of work in the pipeline before he left. They had always told him he was a great worker. They didn't look after all their employees well (keeping them on month-to-month contracts and not giving them the higher salaries that they deserved). This was the type of company that might take you back after making you redundant, but if you decided to resign, you would not easily get a job back with them. They were very nasty in some ways. Because of this we had to pray and ask God to help make this new job work, as we knew that if it didn't, we would be back in a bad situation again where my husband would have no work or opportunities.

We were now in April and things were falling apart. It was not going well for my husband on site and no matter how hard I tried and prayed, nothing seemed to be helping him. It was a possibility he would lose his job. I knew that if this happened now it would break my husband. I didn't know what to do to help him.

'Please, Jesus, help me. I don't know what to do, or how to change things. I NEED HELP, LORD.' This was all I kept praying and asking. 'We need help. The devil is winning, and I can't stop it, no matter how hard I pray, try to change things or comfort my husband.'

A week later and things started to look a little better for my husband. I then prayed to Jesus, to say thank you. But I knew that my husband still needed help on site as things were still very hard for him.

Here We Go Again

Here we were another week later in April 2019, and guess what everything has fallen apart. My husband has been told that once he leaves site, his contract is finished and there is no way that he will be going back. My husband is broken. He is so far away, and I feel terrible for him. He has been given the worst news and now he still has to finish working his rotation on site. There is nothing I can do to comfort him and let him know it's okay, it's not his fault and that he tried his hardest.

I prayed to God and asked, 'Why? Why is it that my husband is always getting hurt with his work? Why does he always get pushed down and made to feel useless? A few years ago he was doing so well. He was always a top employee and he was so happy in his work. It seems that every job just hasn't work out since his first redundancy and this just breaks him down more and more.'

This time I think he has been broken completely. He has lost all self-confidence in himself and his capabilities.

I know he always tries his best with his work, and he said the same. As he was so far away all I could do was pray that Jesus would be with him and help him through the difficult last few weeks he would have left on site, that He would comfort him, and let him know he was not alone, then help us through what might come after this.

Another week on and it's been hard. I'm worried about my husband not having work when he returns. And what about our plans to leave the country? I had to pray to Jesus and ask that he would help my husband, that things on site could change and that they would tell him he could go back for one more rotation. I couldn't see any other way for us to get through things or get our visas sorted.

We have also come to realise that we can't depend on other people to help us in any situations we've faced. It seems that people promise the world, but if you do go to them for help, then there are always ten thousand stories as to why they can't. The truth is that they actually aren't interested in helping. So we have to do things on our own, and with God's help only.

Today is almost the end of April and I was thinking about when my husband would be coming home. I feel lost again, sad and disappointed, I didn't know what was wrong and what was going to happen, and I hated this feeling. Here we are back on that slippery slope again, heading for the dark bottom of that very deep hole. I couldn't see how we were going to get through another hard time with no money and my husband not working. We were still not in a great place financially, so this could be it. This could be where we do end up homeless. No matter how hard I prayed to God asking him to reveal to me what would happen or what we should do, I didn't seem to be getting any answer, not even a sign to point me in the right direction, to let me know that things were going to be okay, All I could do was ask that by some miracle my husband wouldn't lose his job now, that he could go back for one more rotation, as this would give us time to plan, and maybe even get job interviews lined up.

A few days later we were in May. Today there was a problem on my husband's site. The manager asked if he could sort the problem, and for the first time he could tell them confidently exactly what was wrong, what to do to get everything sorted. In the moment that he told me this, I sensed it made him feel better about himself. Thank you, Jesus, for giving my husband a good day, and helping him to know that he is not useless, as he'd had stuck in his head.

Halfway through May and things seem to be improving again. It even looks like my husband could be returning to site for one more rotation. Things on site have been going well, which is great news, and has made us all feel better. Thank you, LORD.

Now, there was another issue my daughter. She had always had a hard time at school, and things were getting harder. I was getting tougher on her too, as I couldn't understand her difficulties. She was having extra classes every day, but nothing seemed to be helping her. She hated school. And she hated doing homework with my mother or me, as we were just way too hard on her and would lose our tempers with her too quickly when she didn't understand. I would look at the work and think to myself, *This is so easy. Why can't she do these things? Why can't she do these simple tasks?* Then one day I had to take a step back and think, *Hold on, she is learning. She doesn't know these things; she is still young and everything they learn at school is new. When all of us start learning about something new, we don't always understand and get it straightaway*. I then tried to remember that she was learning and tried to keep calm when helping her with her homework—no matter how frustrating it would sometimes be. Yes, I would still get angry at times, but I tried hard to see my anger and tried to keep calm.

It seems that when one thing gets better another thing happens so that something else gets worse. All I can do is PRAY. It just seems so wrong; all I do is ask for help—and I know there are people out there in the world in much worse situations than us— but why, oh why, do I have to keep asking? I feel so bad. It just seems that everything that is happening is something I can't fix or deal with without God's help. So, once again, I had to place my daughter's schooling in God's hands and ask that he help her, and help my mother and me to have more patience so that we could help her.

Here we are now at the end of May. Things started off well today, but halfway through, another blow came regarding the visa applications. The only option I would have if we couldn't make up the money we needed for the savings, and if I couldn't get the job offer from the UK before we applied, was that I would have to go over to the UK for a minimum of 6 months, leaving my family behind. I couldn't believe that this would be what God wanted: to split our family up. Please, Lord, here I am again praying for help. Please let my husband be able to go back for one more rotation. Please don't let him lose his job.

While I know you may think 6 months doesn't seem that long, think of all the time that I would miss with my family. While my husband and I were used to his working away for long periods, I had always been there. I couldn't see leaving my children for so long, missing the everyday things—yes, even the things that normally irritated me like homework!

I would be alone in a country that I didn't know, trying to get a job and trying to push to get things sorted, to get the visas. My children would be without a mother. I wouldn't be there if they got ill or hurt. I wouldn't just be able to hold them, put them to bed. This was something I didn't think I could do. It would feel as if I would be walking out of their lives. My children were still very young. What would they think? They would think I had left for ever.

One hundred and eighty days of not being there for the children, a hundred and eighty days to be away from my husband, a hundred and eighty days missing everyday life as a family. One hundred and eighty days, wow! To me this felt like a lifetime when I thought about it. No, no, please, God, don't let this be the only way for us to get the visas. Just thinking of leaving hurts me in a way I can't explain. It makes me feel like I can't breathe. Thinking of the hurt my children would feel, and what they would think of me, was just not something I wanted to go through.

We are now halfway through June and the news we didn't want to hear came today: confirmation that my husband's contract is ending and that his contract will not be renewed. Why, oh Lord, why? What is it that we are doing that is so wrong that this keeps happening?

After the devastating confirmation that my husband was once again not going to have a job, we had to make a hard decision: leave the visa application completely, or use the money my husband had made to push through with the visa application, and use the savings we had to live on until my husband got another job, and the visas were sorted. If we used the savings to live on while my husband was not working, this would mean I would have to try and get a job offer from the UK, or leave and to get a job in the UK, the exact thing I didn't want.

My husband was going to be heading back home soon, and today we had some good news. I have been contacted by a company in the UK to which I'd applied for a job, and they want to do an online interview with me. This was great news. (We needed some good news, as things had been looking against us all the time.)

I had the interview this week for the company in the UK. It was online. I was recorded and had to answer questions on a video. How weird was that! Anyway, my husband was now back home and we have decided that it's now or never. I will have to go to the UK to get a job and work there for 6 months so that we can get the visas sorted. With the way that things were going in our country it would just get worse and harder, so we had to do what we thought was the best for our family and the future.

This was all a little much for me. All at once, I had to face the fact that I had to leave my family behind. And it would not just be 6 months; it would be longer as I would need first to go over to look for a job, then work for 6 months. Only then could we submit the visas. And that could take another 3 months or more. The worst thing was that at the same time my husband had no job and I would have to leave them all here and worry about how we were going to live two separate lives and afford everything.

Even though I was so scared and worried, I knew that this was what God wanted. It's hard to explain, but I just knew that no matter how hard this was going to be, this was the right thing to do.

Just like that, we said it was now all in God's hands. No matter how hard it was, we were going to get ready to leave our country. So we put the house back on the market and I resigned and set my dates to leave for the UK. This was extremely hard. All I could do was pray that God would help us, as we'd now placed this all in his hands and were relying on him completely.

We are now in July and everything is sort of falling into place. I have some family members in the UK who have agreed I can stay with them until I get a job and a place to live. Thank you, God, as this meant I didn't have to book into a hotel for who knew how long. I knew this would be hard for me, as I didn't really know them. (I remember visiting them when I was much younger, but this was over 20 something years ago.) But if that's where God wants me, then I will go. And they were the only family members who were willing to help me at the time.

Picture yourself for a moment on the top of a huge mountain, standing at the very edge. As you look around you can see for miles. It is beautiful, but at the same time you realise that you are all alone. Then the feelings start to rush in: the feeling of fear, worry, then that empty feeling, that feeling of knowing there is nothing around you, you are all alone. When you look around there is nothing for miles and all of a sudden you feel a huge weight on your shoulders that seems to get heavier and heavier. This is how I felt not knowing what I was going to do, or how we were going to make it through. All I could keep doing was pray, 'Please Lord, please God, please help me and my family to make it through what is to come.'

I had to start praying that God would give me the right job as soon as possible so that I could start working no later than September. 'PLEASE HELP ME, LORD.'

Everyone had said I didn't need to worry, there was lots of work in the UK and I could do any kind of job and earn a good salary. The only problem was that I had to earn a certain amount for the visa application.

The Beginning of the Worst Time of My Life

We were now at the end of July and today was the last day at work. While I was excited and happy that this day had finally come, I was also worried, as there was no turning back now. And when you think about it, I guess we were crazy doing all this just because we thought it was what God wanted, that we had to trust him and that we'd just placed everything in his hands. All we had to do was keep believing and hoping that we were doing what we thought was right.

As I drove out of my office parking area for the last time, I was thinking to myself, *This is the last time I will ever see this place.* I then started to feel my heart breaking. Fear, anxiety and worry flooded over me. But as this started, I said out aloud, 'I am ready, Lord. I am ready for the next step in this journey.' (I could only do it with His help and guidance.)

Then as I drove out of the office park, a car turned in front of me, and I looked at the number plate which showed: JESUS LU. Wow, thank you, Jesus, for letting me know that you are there and that we are in this together!

Two days later I had an online interview with a recruitment company in the UK. I told Jesus that if they had the right job for me this would be great, but we would have to wait and see.

The hardest part for me through the interview was to understand what the people were saying, as the accent was something totally different to what I was used to hearing. I just hoped I'd done okay.

We were now at the start of August. The time was coming close for me to leave. I would be leaving my family on the 10th of August 2019 and I was feeling worried and scared. That same feeling came back into my mind again where I'm on top of that very high mountain, where the weight is just pushing down on me and there is nothing I can do, and there was no way out and I didn't know how this would end, and I was all alone.

Today one of my mother's good Christian friends came to visit. She said that she had to speak to me, as she had a message for me before I leave. She said that Jesus had given her a message. I know if you don't believe in Jesus, or have any faith, it's hard to understand when you hear people say they have a message from God, or Jesus spoke to them. It's important to understand that it's not always as it sounds: you hear a clear voice that says, do this or say this. Most of the time we get little messages in dreams, pictures, or verses. Or it's just raw gut feelings that let you know that you have to do something. Although, yes, sometimes you do get a clear spoken message in a dream or from another person. A person who has faith will understand that this message is not a normal feeling, or a dream, and you as the person will know that it is from Jesus, and that you have a duty to give that message to a person or people.

What I'm trying to explain is the occasion when I told you how things had worked out; when I spoke about my husband's sister and mother that one day when they came over; how everything just fell into place; where we were all alone, and faith was discussed. When we discussed what we'd been through and how we got through things, and how I felt at the time. I knew I had to say things, that at the time the whole situation felt different. I knew at that time it was a message that I needed to give to them, and it could have been just one word I said, or how we all felt in that time, that they needed to hear or feel something, and that would have been a message for them from God. Sometimes when you hear or see things, you get this feeling that it was aimed at you, or it was meant for you. This is sometimes how we are guided through faith and know that we are not alone. Or we get the answers we have been waiting for.

When she started talking, I started crying. I didn't know why, but I couldn't stop it, no matter how hard I tried. Sitting there on the bed, she said to me that God was my father, I may not have had a good earthly father, but God was my father. He had always been there and would always be there. All I needed to do was ask and believe and He would be there to answer my prayers and help me. The verse she had given me was Jeremiah 29:11. 'He promises us a future filled with success and not of suffering.' (New King James Version) She then said that God would open all the doors we needed to make this move successful. All we had to do was trust God. And she then said that my family would be with me in the UK soon.

After speaking to her I felt a little better, knowing that we were doing the right things and that Jesus was there and was going to help us through this.

A few days later and the day had now arrived. Tonight I get on a plane and leave my family behind to try and get things sorted out for us in the UK. Trust me, this is the worst feeling ever. I had to try hard not to cry and break down all day long in front of my children. I had to be strong. I had to keep telling them it wouldn't be long, even though I knew that was not true, as I knew it would be months, but I just tried to hold them and we had a good day together as a family. At the time it felt almost like I was saying goodbye forever, but at the same time I knew it would not be. The day felt long. It was hard to try and act happy when at the back of my mind, I knew by the end of the day I would be leaving.

I didn't want the children to go with me to the airport because I knew how hard it was when my husband left for work. They would cry all the way home, and I knew that I could not keep myself together saying goodbye at the airport and seeing them cry. I knew that would break me.

I knew that if I said goodbye at home, they would feel comforted, as my mother was there, and they could be distracted with TV or something else quickly, so the tears would not be as bad. It was just easier to say goodbye at home.

When we got to the airport, I didn't want to go, I started doubting that what I was doing was the right thing, but at the same time I knew that we had passed the point of no return months ago, and no matter how I felt or how hard it was or what lay ahead, I had to do this for my family.

The time was now here. I kissed my husband goodbye and walked through the check-in gates, trying to distract myself so I wouldn't cry. I waved one last time and headed through to the passport control. Here I go all on my own, I am going to need Jesus to help me through this. My heart was breaking inside as I stood in the long queue. I started looking around, trying hard to distract myself, looking at all the people around me. Most people were in groups, as families, couples, or friends, and here I was lost in this sea of people all alone.

When I finally landed in the UK, I was tired, as I couldn't sleep on the plane, but I couldn't wait to get a SIM card so that I could contact my family. Before I'd left my country, we'd set up roaming on my phone, so I couldn't wait to let my husband know that I was safe.

Normally when you travel, you look forward to walking out of the airport and meeting your family or friends, knowing that when you get out of the airport your holiday will start. You get excited and filled with happiness. Well, my feelings were the total opposite. When I walked out, I was nervous. I had to find people who were family, but I didn't know them. I would have to try make small talk with people I didn't know. I didn't know what to expect, and I would have to do this for who knew how long, so all I felt was dread as I walked towards the doors.

When we were travelling to their house, which was about a two-hour drive from the airport, we just spoke about my journey and how they were, and what they had done for all these years. While we were driving along, I tried to get my phone to work on roaming, but it was not working and it was so frustrating. All I wanted was to send a message to my husband to say I was safe, and I think a huge part of me just wanted to see a message back from him.

We had arranged with my aunt a while back that she would get a UK SIM card for me so that I could put a UK phone number on my CV. So I asked if she had brought it with her. However, she said she'd left it at home. She also said that later that evening we would be going out for dinner. To be honest, I was just so tired. All I really wanted to do was be on my own and talk to my family. I hadn't had a direct flight to the UK; I'd had to fly via Dubai and unfortunately, I'm one of those people who can't sleep on a plane, so by this time I was physically and mentally drained, as some of you might understand.

My heart was broken from leaving my family, and again here I was, trying to act like nothing was wrong. It was hard talking to people I didn't really know and acting like everything was great when inside all I wanted to do was go home, feeling that I might burst out crying. Anyway, we got to their house, and I was given the SIM card, so I was finally able to let my husband know that

I was safe. I was able to say hello to my children too. Shortly after that I had to get ready to go out for dinner. When we got back to my aunt's house after dinner, it was still early, but I said that I was tired, and I went to my room. I just wanted to be on my own and have the opportunity to talk to my family again.

The days passed, I had now been in the UK for a week, and I am feeling down. I feel like everything is standing still. All I wanted to do was come over, get a job, start working, and get a place for us to live, just get everything moving as fast as possible, but the opposite seems to be happening. It's almost like everything around me has been paused.

I had to go to Preston on my own to apply for my national insurance number. This was a little scary for me, just because I'm not used to using a train as transport and had no idea where I had to go, or what to expect. However, it was a nice two-hour train trip looking at the English countryside as it flew by. Looking out of the train window, everything appeared so clean, green, and calm. We lived just outside of a huge city back home, so everything was always so busy and there was not much green around.

When I arrived in Preston and had found the place I needed to go, while I was waiting, I got a call about the job in Penrith. Now this was the interview I'd had online when I was still back in my country months ago. This was a call I hadn't expected. They advised me that I had a face-to-face interview on the following Monday. Thank you, Jesus, for opening the doors as you had promised. I prayed that I would get the job, as I would need to start working by September.

Monday came. I was excited and nervous about the job interview, and I knew that this had to be the job that Jesus had planned for me, as this was the job I'd applied for when I was back in my home country—where I'd had the odd online interview in which I'd had to answer questions while being recorded. To be honest I couldn't wait to take that next important step on this journey to start working and to start the 6 months countdown.

Well, after the interview I was disappointed. I'd had the normal face-to-face meeting and questions, then I'd had to take a test, a knowledge test. WHAT! you know how stressed you are for an interview, and now they expect you to write a test as well. I have never had an interview like this before. It was definitely not anything like our interviews back home. Afterwards, I was told in an odd way that I was not really what they wanted. The salary being offered was not very good nor the same as on the job offer that I'd had read. To be honest, in a way, during the whole interview, I knew that I was not what they wanted. Sometimes in an interview you can just feel if the person likes you or not. I thought this had been the job that God had planned for me, but after this interview I guess I was wrong. However, even though the interview didn't go that well, I still prayed that God would keep that door open. If that was the job he wanted for me, then they would come back to me with a job offer, and the salary would be what I required for the visas.

The following day I was contacted by another company for an interview. This time it was in Manchester. The train journey was a little more stressful this time, as Manchester was a bigger city and I had to walk to the interview from the station. When I'd looked at the map before travelling, it hadn't looked that far to walk. I'd seen that I would have to cross the middle of town, and I know this doesn't sound that bad, but I had no idea where I was going. All I could do at the time was follow my phone. It was all so busy and some streets were closed off as there was a Pride parade going on. It all felt a little overwhelming with cars and buses, tall buildings, people all over. And then there were small dirty streets where there were no people at all.

I had not been in a big city for a while. The last one had been back home. I hated the cities. They were always so busy and felt dark because of the high buildings. It was also a dirty and dangerous place to be. People would get hijacked when waiting at traffic lights, and the cities were known danger zones if you ended up in the wrong area. You would never walk down a lonely street on your own.

I immediately felt the old feeling of fear creeping back into my mind, looking and scanning as I was walking, trying to just make sure no one was too close to me or following on behind. I had no idea what to expect, or what the dangers were in this city. I just felt the old fears in me that I had back in my country walking in the city, and what made it just a little worse was, I knew I was walking through the streets alone. I remember at one stage my phone had sent me into a little side street. I was concentrating so hard on where to go, and with all the traffic, when I looked up, there was no one, just me in this lonely street, which smelt like dead fish and old oil. I walked as fast as possible and tried to keep an eye on everything around me. I finally found the building where my interview was, and I went in and waited.

Knowing what to expect this time, I had the interview and the test. But while the salary was good—and enough for the visa application—this was only a year's contact. They wanted people to assist in moving policies from one system onto another. In my head this was not really what I wanted, but a job for a year was better than nothing and maybe this was what God wanted for me.

A week later, I heard back from the Manchester job that I was not successful. In a way it was a disappointment, but, on the other hand I was happy, just thinking that I didn't have to do the hours of travelling and having to work in the city.

We were now at the end of August. I was worried because I needed to start working from the first of September. I hadn't heard anything back from the Penrith job, but I guess they did say that I hadn't got it. I knew that I was not going to make my deadline of getting a job by September. I know that everything happens in God's time and His time is different from ours, but I just didn't know what God's plans were, as my hopes were now fading by the hour, and thoughts of failure started to get to me. I prayed to God to please help me and let me know what his plans were.

I would sit day in and day out looking at jobs, and applying for jobs. I was not only looking in the area I stayed, but I was also looking from one end of the UK to the other, and yes, I was getting desperate. Every day I would keep looking and applying until it came to the point where there was nothing, no new jobs that I hadn't already seen, or applied for. I had even started looking at work in supermarkets, and cafés. I knew that the salaries in these jobs were not close to what I needed for our visas, but I just thought if I had to do two or three jobs just to get to the correct amount, then I would.

I walked into town one day. I was surprised to see that here it was still the old way of advertising a job: if they had a vacancy, they would have a notice up in the window. I was in town from opening time: 9 am. I walked down every street and looked at every window of every place that had a note up. I handed in my CV to each one. As the day was coming to an end—it was now about 4 pm—I went into a café that had a note up showing an opening. They told me to come in and sit down to wait to see the manager. As I sat down at a table at the back of the café, I realised it had been the first time I'd sat down or taken a break all day. In that moment I realised that my feet were so sore from being on them all day and that I was tired.

Eventually the manager came. She sat down and asked me a few questions and I answered. Then she took my CV and said she would get back to me. I thanked her for taking the time to speak to me, and she got up and left. I looked at the time and thought I should start heading back to the house.

As I got up, the pain in my feet was terrible I didn't even know how I was going to make it back to the house. I didn't have the money to pay for a taxi or take a bus, so I had to just push through and walk. Halfway back to the house, there was another café. I thought I really needed to sit down and take a break, so I went in and had something to drink. I thought the whole day had been a waste. I knew that none of the places I'd been to would take me on. I felt that the people in most of the places I'd been to saw me as a foreigner. I got the feeling they would rather employ a British person. I could understand this, but at the same time wished that someone would just give me a chance.

Today was the 14th of September 2019. In my journal I have been keeping a verse that was given to me when leaving my country:

> Jeremiah 29:11 – 'I know the plans I have for you,' says the Lord. 'They are plans to prosper you and not to harm you, plans to give you hope and a future.'

> (New King James Version)

Reading this, I'd been hoping that it would be a good day, but it was the opposite. I still had no work. All I was doing was crying myself to sleep every night, and my heart was breaking. I was lost, I missed my family, and I had no idea what to do. And Jesus was not answering my prayers.

All I could do was keep praying and hope that things would change soon. Every day that passed felt like it was taking forever. There were no more jobs to apply for, and no calls for interviews. I had hit a dead end, and it was a terrible sinking feeling I had.

My bedroom window looked out onto a field. When I first arrived, I saw that the field had been almost ready to be harvested. At that time, I'd thought to myself that by the time it was ready to harvest, I would not be there to see it. But as I looked out of the window this morning, I saw they had already started. There were now huge bails in the field. So then I thought to myself, *Before they gather the bales, I will be out of this temporary place and have a home for my family and me.*

Guess what? It's another week later, and I had the best call, the call I have been praying for. I was just offered the job in Penrith. However, I made a huge mistake. Before even thinking, I accepted the salary. But this was not enough to cover the requirements for the visas, so the stress is not over. I still now need to find a second job. How stupid I was! I had been so desperate and when I'd got the call, I think my mind was just in a state of shock.

Then guess what? I got another call, for another job interview—down in Huntington. This is where my husband's older sister lives and they've said I can come down to visit for a week. But what was I going to do? I had a job offer that I'd just accepted, but the salary was not enough. I also had this other interview, but who knows if I would get it. At that moment I didn't know what job God wanted for me.

I decided to go for the interview in Huntington. I felt it wouldn't hurt and I needed a break from the place I was staying. I was still so angry with myself for making the mistake of accepting a salary that was not going to be enough for the visas (and I couldn't even find a temporary job that would make up the difference in salary either).

The situation with the family where I was staying was also becoming fragile. They kept making remarks outside my door, things like, 'I don't know when she will leave' and 'I know it's been long enough now' and 'It's been longer than two weeks.'

To be honest, I hadn't made the arrangements for staying with them; my mother had helped with that, as she knew them better than I did. Owing to the remarks being made, however, I did ask my mother if she'd told them I would only be staying for two weeks, but she said no. She told me they'd said I could stay as long as I wanted or needed to.

When I had first arrived, I would clean the house, and do the dishes and washing, trying to help as a way of pay for my board (even though I did give them a small amount of money for letting me stay with them). However, they didn't like me doing things, and they would always have something negative to say about what I did to try and help. Because of this I stopped doing things and just tried to keep to myself, keep things clean and tidy where I went. To be honest, I would be in my room most of the time. Only in the evenings would I come down, sit a while before and after dinner, then go up, bath and go to bed. At the time I thought it would be better to stay out the way, as they were used to their own space. If I wasn't around much, I thought it might help make the situation better.

I travelled down by train to my husband's sister's place and went for the other interview. This went well. I was not nervous at all. I felt comfortable. And the people who conducted the interview were a lot more welcoming than any I'd had before. The week's trip to my husband's sister did me good. I felt a little better, felt a little stronger again. In that week I'd felt like I belong and I was happier. They had accepted me being around them. But this feeling disappeared the minute I saw my uncle when he collected me from the train station on my return. I knew more than ever now that I was not actually welcome, they didn't want me around. But I had nowhere else to go.

On the drive back to the house, I was also starting to get a little worried. I'd still had no official offer from the Penrith job. This was 2 weeks down the line from when they'd originally called to say that I had the job. Funny how in a moment I was back to feeling the world was on my shoulders again, how the sadness had taken over. You think, how can things change in the blink of an eye? I'd felt happier and stronger a second ago, but a moment later the sky had turned dark and I was back to feeling my heart breaking as I sensed the hatred around me. I had no idea what I was going to do, or what God's plans were.

The following day I got news that I hadn't got the job in Huntington. They said I was too confident and would suit a sales job better. I was reaching breaking point. I was starting to fall apart. I don't know how to explain this, but if you have ever been through hard times you may understand.

Since I'd arrived in the UK, I would wake up every morning hoping for the best, praying that today would be the day that everything would come together and things would change. But as each day went on, the weight on my shoulders would become heavier and heavier. And the days seemed longer, just to get me down even more. By the time night came, I could hardly keep back the tears. When I went to bed, I would read one of my faith books, hoping that I would feel better or get an answer to what was happening. I would look at the pictures of my children and my husband, and I could no longer fight back the tears.

I would start crying, and I would cry for hours. All I could think was, *How are my family? What are they doing? Did they have a good day?* When I spoke to them every night, it was really hard, as I would try only to be positive and act as if everything was good. But at night in bed the hurt would build up. I'd left my children. I'd left my husband. And for what? For everything to fall apart? I felt like it was all my fault and no matter how hard I was trying, I just seemed to be failing.

The hurt I was feeling was indescribable. It felt literally like my heart was breaking. I had to make sure that no one could hear me crying in my room at night, until eventually in the early hours of the morning I would fall asleep, only to wake up a few hours later and the whole process would start again.

I had to send an email to the visa company and ask if there was another way of getting the visas, because I didn't think I was going to be able to get a job, as I still had no contact or documents from the job in Penrith. I now thought that they'd just played a sick joke on me. All the employment websites still had the same jobs advertised and I had already applied to them all. There was nothing new, no positive news or interviews. Everything just seemed to come to an end. Maybe we'd been wanting this too badly, that this was not Gods' plan, and we'd just made a huge mistake.

I didn't think I could keep going. I had been thinking that it was time to say enough is enough and return to South Africa to try and start over somehow. However, we were so deep into this situation now. My husband was not working, as he had to be there to be with the children. We had no home as this had been sold, so they were now living with a family friend. The children were no longer in school, as I was meant to have already started working, we should have already started our 6-month countdown for the visas, but nothing had worked out as planned. So if I did go back now, it would still be a hard situation, so I have to try to hang in there and hope that the job in Penrith comes through. I had finally made contact with the lady who'd made me the offer. They kept saying that the job was mine, but they were having problems and couldn't send me the contract yet.

I still had the other problem in that the salary was not enough, so I needed a second job. That was even worse, as I couldn't even get a job in a store as a cleaner or packer.

We are now in the second week on October 2019, and things are just getting worse. The visa company have come back and said that if I do work two jobs, our countdown can only start when I have been working in both jobs for 6 months. And they would have to be permanent jobs; I couldn't do any work that was part-time or one whereby you are called if they need extra people and you get paid per hour.

So here I was past the deadline we'd had, no further than when I'd first come over. I couldn't find a job. I thought I'd had one, but it just wasn't coming through. I couldn't find even a simple entry level job, like a cleaner, and my aunt and uncle didn't want me here anymore. I actually don't know what to do or how long I could go on in this way.

One night I had to tell God, I couldn't do this anymore, I was reaching my breaking point. If I'd made a mistake by coming to the UK, why had he opened this door for us? Why did things happen to help get us here? Why would he let nothing work out for us, and why would he now close all the doors? Why was he hurting my family and me like this? Was it all just to teach me a hard lesson, was it to break me but at the same time ripping me apart, and ruining my family? I handed everything to God again and asked him to take control because I couldn't do it anymore. I was falling apart, my heart was broken, my faith was dwindling, and I was finding it hard to even keep myself together. After that prayer I closed my eyes and fell asleep.

The following day I got a call for an interview the following week. I knew this was my last chance to get a job with the salary I needed. I immediately thought this was the answer to my prayers.

My Dream

In the early hours of this morning I had a dream. In it I could see myself in different places, my family with me. Then it would change. But in every picture there was a person in white. You couldn't see a face, or actual skin, as the light was too bright from the figure. The light was so bright that all you could make out was that it was a figure of a man. Then everything in my dream went quiet, dead quiet. I was standing on a street with houses along it, but all the houses were white and the house windows gave off the softest yellow glow. At the same time there were street lights giving off an even brighter light. Everything was calm and quiet. I felt peaceful standing alone on this street.

I was then standing looking across the street. And on the other side was a row of houses with a street light and a railing. The bright glowing figure that I'd seen earlier was on the other side. Then a voice spoke through the silence saying, 'It's time for me to go.' I looked across at the figure and in my mind I asked, *Will I ever see you again?* and *Why are you leaving me?*

At this point the bright figure was moving further away down the street. Then in a flash, I could see his face right in front of me, and I looked into his eyes for a moment. Then it went back to being the far away bright figure that had now turned and looked back in my direction. The voice said, 'I'm always with you.' And just like that the dream ended.

I cannot explain the feeling I had in that dream, but I will try:

It was a feeling of pure calm. There was nothing: no noise, no people, cars, animals, nothing moving. It was just me in a street with lights and houses. I hadn't felt scared, and the light was beautiful, the type I've never seen before. It had felt like I was home, where I needed to be.

When the voice spoke it was calming, and when the figure walked away, just for a moment I had this feeling rush over me of uncertainty, of what now, why you are leaving me? But as that happened and I looked into that face and those eyes, when that figure walked away and said 'I'm always with you', the uncertainty was washed away; it disappeared.

I opened my eyes. For a moment my eyes had to adjust, as the room was dark. At that moment I thanked God, thanked Him for letting me know that I was not alone, and that everything was going to be okay, that things would work out.

My mother's Christian friend, who'd prayed for me before I left my country, shared that her prayer team had prayed for me to have success at the interview I was going to have the following day. She said that a lady in her team had seen a big glass door opening as they were praying, and she hoped that this would mean something to me. This made me feel excited because this was also the first time I'd asked people to pray for me, and for my family.

Unfortunately, Tuesday came and the interview was a total disaster. I sat in huge boardroom, there were five people who all had a turn asking me different questions, giving me scenarios that I had to respond to. While I could answer all the questions on insurance, I couldn't answer the questions on the UK laws and how things worked in the UK insurance industry. In the back of my mind I knew this job would have been an answer to our prayers—the salary was a lot more than we needed and would have made many things easier—but that was one of the worst interviews I'd ever had in my life. When I left and started my walk back to the train all I could tell myself was that this was all in God's hands. He is the only one that can work miracles.

We were now on the 23rd of October, and today I was contacted by the Penrith job again. I'd decided a few days back to email the lady who'd offered me the job to ask if they would increase the salary to the amount I needed for the visas. As they'd been keeping me waiting this long for an actual contract, I thought I could but ask the question.

The manager replied, asking me to supply proof of the amounts I needed for the visas. It was only a small additional amount I required. I therefore asked the visa agency to provide me with a letter stating the total annual salary required for the visas and sent this through to them as proof. Now all I could do was pray again that Jesus would help me and that they would accept the details and increase my salary.

A day later, she came back to me and agreed to increase my salary to the amount required. And then she confirmed that I would have my contract in the next few days. When I read this email from them, I was so relieved, as it meant I didn't have to worry about finding an additional job. I could now move on and start to think about what I needed to do next.

I spent the next week walking around in the small town trying to find a cheap car, which I finally found. The car was very old and didn't look the best, but I thought it would have to do for now; I just needed to be able to get to and from work. I didn't like having to rely on my aunt and uncle, who were already not happy with me being there, so asking for a lift was also not nice, so I just ended up walking everywhere. A car would give me that little bit of independence, and I could now start looking for properties to rent.

Thank you, Lord. I know that we still have a long way to go, but things are finally starting to move in the right direction. (I was still not past all the crying at night because I missed my family; the last three months had been the darkest and worst months of my life)

I know three months doesn't seem that long, but knowing the whole family's lives and futures depended on you, knowing every passing day was another we all had to be apart; suffering the consequences of our decision, knowing that if I failed, we would all fail, that I would have to go back to my country, and we would be on the streets homeless with nothing, everything we'd been through the last few years and months would have been for nothing, and I would have ruined our lives forever, it was a lot of stress and worry to carry, knowing that it was all on my shoulders. We were now way over the time limit we had originally given ourselves. I thought that by now we would have been halfway through our 6 months, but we now just had to try and hang in there and push through. I needed the contract to come through for the job so that I could start working.

We were now at the start of November 2019. I'd finally got my contract for the job in Penrith and I was hoping to start as soon as possible. But there was going to be a delay, they said, as they needed to process a few things, I know you who are reading this might wonder why was I so worried about a day, or a month's delay, but every day was a delay to when our 6-month countdown would start, and this was a big thing for us, as it would mean an extra day or extra month away from being together as a family again, and a longer time that we have to survive on the savings we had. We knew the money would run out, as costs were high, and there had been no income since August.

Our original plan from the start was to have my husband and the children fly over and stay with me for 6 months on a visitor visa. The children would be home schooled during this period. In this way we wouldn't be apart for so long. So we had originally booked the flights for the first week in December. They would have stayed until January 2020. However this plan had depended on me starting work in September. We'd worked out that they could return to our country in January and apply for the visas. But with everything delayed, we would have to fly them back in January, then apply for another set of 6-month visas, and they would then have to fly back to the UK again. The cost of visitor visas, flying back and forth, along with the cost of living was all going to take huge amounts out of our savings very quickly, and we had to make sure that we would still have enough to pay for the big application for the family visas.

I was also having a hard time finding a place to rent. Because I was not actually working yet and was new to the country, no one was giving me the opportunity to rent. Even when I assured them that I had my job and showed them the paperwork which proved I had the deposit and rent amount, still they all came back and said no, sorry I couldn't rent the property. Here we go, another situation to worry about. My family would be arriving in a few weeks' time and now I would have no place for them to stay, so we would have to arrange to stay in a B&B, another additional cost, which we actually could not afford. I was worried, as I knew my family could not stay with me at my aunt and uncle's. They'd already said in a roundabout way that they would not be welcome in their house.

I have now been away from my family for 3 months, and it just seems that every step forward seems to take forever. And every time things look as if they are heading in the right direction, it feels like a door gets slammed in our faces, or a huge mountain comes into our path just to make the journey harder and longer.

The time apart, and the delays and issues we'd had in the past 3 months were starting to take a toll on us all. I feel terrible about everything and all I can do is hope and pray that one day our children will understand why we had to do this. I know when they are older, they will probably not remember, but here and now, they are angry, sad and don't understand why we are doing this to them. They didn't understand that the way things were going for us, that if we'd stayed in our country, we would be homeless and we would not have been able to look after them.

Again here I am, with no one to turn to, or speak to. I can't even speak to my husband, because I have to maintain the act of being positive and happy, as I didn't want him worrying about me. I wanted and needed him there to support the children. So, God, here I am again. I ask please that you take this situation of finding a place to rent into your hands and hear my prayers for help.

Moving on Slowly

Today was the 4th of November 2019. Today my uncle said that I have to be out their house permanently by the end of the month. He said they wanted to have family over, but as I had been there for so long, they'd had to say no to everyone. I could no longer stay, as they wanted other people to come and visit now. In that moment I wondered how could this keep happening. Just when I thought we were moving forward, and I'd started thinking that we were climbing out of the deep black hole (as I now had a job), something else happened to knock me back down. And it breaks me all over again.

I have tried so hard to keep positive. From the day I arrived I tried my best not to be in their way. I'd helped clean the house, do washing, as I know how hard it is living with other people. When you have someone come into your home, it is hard to accept and adapt, so I tried my best to keep a low profile. But this didn't help. Here I was again, standing at the foot of a huge mountain, looking up and thinking now what, how will I get over this mountain in the time I have.

I was waiting to finally start working the following week. Two weeks later my family were due to arrive, but now I had to find a place to stay, a place for us to live. I had less than a month to do this, and no one would rent a property to me.

I think that my aunt and uncle believe that I wasn't looking for a place, or that I was being too picky. Or maybe they thought I didn't want to move out, but it was all the total opposite. I wanted desperately to move out, and if I could have done it all in one day, I would have. I was willing to take any property, but things just didn't want to work out for me.

I had to ask God what had I done that was so bad that I must be punished this way? Why? Please tell me so that I can fix it, so that I don't pull my whole family into this endless dark pit with me. It was not fair that my family were being punished for my sins and mistakes.

I was finally happy to know that I was going to start working soon, but at the same time was taking another knock by being told to get out with nowhere to go. And my family were coming soon. Please, Lord, help me! I need a miracle again. I had to believe that God would not let this all fall apart now, just when things were starting to move forward.

I start working on the 11th of November. This meant that I had 4 full days left to try and find a place to stay. I had to pray that in this time I could find somewhere, because once I'd started working there would be no time to go out and look at places, except on weekends. My time was running out fast.

I went to see a place late one afternoon. It was not in a fantastic area, and it had been raining the whole day, so everything looked a little gloomy. It was a small property. This time I was not meeting an agent; it was the owner of the property who showed me around. After the viewing, I told him of my situation, that I was due to start working in the next few days, and I confirmed I had the deposit and the first month's rent. I told him that so far everyone had said no to renting me a property, as I hadn't started working and hadn't rented in the UK before. When I asked if he would be willing to give me a chance, he looked at me and said, 'That's so silly, how could everyone have said no? We all have to start somewhere.' He then said he was willing to give me that opportunity and If I wanted to rent the house I could. Thank you, Lord. Thank you for helping me with the situations I was facing. In that moment it seemed things were starting to look better, even though it was stressful to get to that point.

Today was the 8th of November 2019. As I was due to start work soon, I contacted the people who were helping us with our visas to confirm that I was starting my new job and that I had a place for us to live, and then to confirm when we could submit our visa application. As I spoke to the agent, my heart started breaking a little again, as now we could only submit in June 2020. I knew we had to wait 6 months, but when you hear someone else confirm the actual dates it just seems more real. And it felt like a lifetime. I was not sure how I could get through such a long time without my family, as we couldn't really afford the flying back and forth, but I had to try to stay positive. Things were slowly moving in the right direction. And with God all things are possible.

My first week in the new job was over and on the 16th of November I moved into our new place. It was not the best but would do for now, and the best thing was, that soon my family would arrive and I could see them and hold them again. We were planning on applying for another 6-month visitor visa for my husband and the children, even if we couldn't really afford it, as this way we could stay together while we waited for the 6 months to pass. They would still have to go back to apply for the subsequent visitor visas and return again to our home country to submit for the main visas, but for now all we had to do was sort out home schooling for my daughter (my son was only 4 years old at the time, so he didn't need to be in school yet).

Two weeks later. I am so excited. Today my children and husband arrive. I had to travel to Newcastle airport, and I was a little nervous about getting there. I had no idea where to go, but at the same time I didn't care, I had a GPS. I was going to leave early to make sure that I would be there in time, and if I got lost or had problems on the road, I didn't need to worry. At the same time I was a little worried because our house was very empty. I had bought some camping chairs for us to sit on, and I could only afford to get inflatable mattresses for sleeping. It really looked like a very poor person's house, a little sad with nothing in it. However, I tried my best to make it look okay and thought I'd make it out to be an adventure for the children when they arrived.

When I arrived at the airport, I was very early, but it was okay. Finally the boards showed that their plane had landed. A while after that, the doors opened and I could see my husband and children standing waiting for their bags. In the split second that the doors opened, my heart stopped. I saw my children and my husband, but they didn't see me waiting, as they were busy. Then the doors opened again and they saw me. Both my children ran towards me. It was the best feeling that I'd had felt for some time: real happiness. Holding onto my children was so comforting and really made me happy deep in my heart. Finally my husband had gathered all the bags together and he too could come through the doors. It felt so good to have our family back together. It felt as if we'd been apart for years, but it had only been just over 3 months.

Time seems to have flown by. Christmas has come and gone and here we were on the 14th of January 2020, the day my husband and children had to return to South Africa.

Now I was all alone again, and it just feels wrong. Being alone again, all the stress and worries have come back to me. All the money we'd saved up was now running extremely low. We didn't know if we could get another set of visitor visas again and the costs of flying to and fro might be something we just can't afford. Once again here I was asking God again to take all the stress, worries and bad situations back into his hands. I also prayed that God remove and close all evil open doors in our new home and in our lives, as it seems each time things improve, something always happens to come and ruin it.

Today was the 28th of January. My husband applied for another 6-month visitor visa for them all. The Embassy called to ask him a whole lot of questions as to why he wanted another set of visas so soon. So now we just have to wait and see if they will process them or not. At the same time my workload has gone out of control and

I am falling behind. I know I should say something, but I'm so scared, as I can't afford to lose my job. I'm also still in my probation period.

A day later and we await the visitor visa news. My work situation turns out not to be as bad as I'd thought, so this day is slightly better, a day when I feel I can take a breath, but only a little, as we were still waiting for the outcome of the visitor visas.

A few hours later and the day just got better. We got the further 6-month visitor visas. (Thank you, Lord!) This was fantastic news as it meant my husband could get the visas in one day, and if it all worked out, my family would be back with me soon. All we would need to do was book the flights.

Two days later, and I feel that the devil is out to get me in this new job. Everything seems to go wrong. Just as one thing gets better, something else happens to knock me back down.

I know that starting a new job is never easy; you always have a target on your back, and you get blamed for basically everything that does go wrong, but things seem so much harder. The people are nice, but at the same time they whisper in corners. I know they help me but then complain to someone else later. They all think I don't hear or know what's going on, so it's a little frustrating and depressing, as I need this job and can't lose it now. I can't see why God would put me here only for me to lose my job.

At the same time our finances are falling apart. We have no more savings and are now using the money we need for the main visa applications. I can't see any way out of this mess at the moment and everything is just falling apart again. I know that we shouldn't worry and that Jesus will help us, He will make a way, but at this moment it just feels like the devil has got his claws in and is ripping everything to pieces.

Delays

Here we are now, the 2nd of February 2020. My family was meant to be flying out today, but at around lunchtime I got a message from my husband saying they were not coming. They can't. I thought he was just joking (as he always likes to joke around with things). I was then stuck in a meeting and I saw I had a few missed calls from him. I immediately called him back, and my heart sank. I could hear by his voice that this was no joke; they were not coming. They had messed up the children's visas. My husband couldn't talk long as he was busy trying to sort things out at the airport, but they could not fly. See, another knock, another door slammed in our faces, another slip back into the black hole.

We were all broken. I could hear my children in the background when I spoke to my husband just saying, 'Why, Daddy?' I wanted just to sit and cry, but I was at work so had to try pull myself together and carry on. It was the hardest thing to do. All I could think about was my husband and children. What was happening? What would happen now with flights? Would we have to pay again? I wondered how the children were. They must be devastated and wouldn't understand. How could the visa people make a mistake? This was all running through my head. All I wanted was to talk to my husband, find out what had happened and what was going to happen now, but here I was stuck at my desk, trying to work when my family were going through a hard time and I couldn't do anything about it.

That evening, I spoke to my husband, he said that when they'd issued the children's visas, they had messed up by getting one digit of husband's passport number wrong. Because of this they could not leave. This meant more problems and delays as my husband had to take everything back to the visa office for them to correct the mistake.

A few days later they had fixed the children's documents and they could fly out again. The best thing was that we didn't have to pay for the flights again; the airline assisted us with our situation.

Today was the 7th of February 2020 and a good day. My family were due to be flying out that night. I was also told that my probation period was over and I was now permanent. What a relief! A good day. And tomorrow morning my family were going to be back with me, and I couldn't wait. Finally, we were going to be back together as a unit.

It is now the 20th of March 2020, and things were going well. But now there is a coronavirus going around the world and so many people are dying. I was now worried about what would happen if any of us became ill. What would we do? And what if my family had to go back to our old country and became ill there? We were just hoping and praying that, as the virus was getting worse all over the world, it would mean that my husband and children couldn't fly back, and that we would be able to do our visa applications from the UK.

However, at the same time, living expenses were high and the savings we had for the main visa applications was getting used day by day. I had no idea how we would be able to make this money up so that we could still afford to apply for the visas. Please, Lord, we are going to need your help again. Please, Lord, please continue to keep your strong rooms open with your blessings, miracles and our finances in this situation we are in at the moment.

Five days later. Owing to the virus, we were all sent home today and advised that we will have to work from home. This was a problem for me as I had no internet at home. It would mean another additional cost that I couldn't really afford at the time. But to keep my job I had to get this sorted.

For the first 3 weeks I was at home but couldn't work as I had to wait for the internet to be installed. It was a nice break as I could spend the time with my family. I was also still getting paid because it was an unexpected event having to make everyone work from home, and they couldn't say anything to me about not having internet at home. It had also given me an idea about how to make up the amount we would need for the visas. I could apply for a credit card. However, because of the virus and the country going into lockdown, there was no answer when I called the bank. So once again I don't know what to do to get extra money together.

However, we received some great news today. The virus that was causing havoc in the world, meant that countries were not allowing travel, and our visa agents confirmed that we qualified to do the main visa applications from within the UK. The only issue now was that normally for the spousal visa, you have to go for a TB test. With everything closed, I had no idea how we could do this and what the costs would be. Here I was once again asking God to help, to hand this over to Him, as I had no idea what we could do to get this test done when everything was closed.

While I knew this virus was bad and so many people were losing their lives all over the world every day, I was happy; for us it was a blessing in disguise, as the virus made it possible for us as a family to stay together in the UK. So I still had to thank Jesus for our situation, even though it was bad for the world, because it was helping us as a family.

Today is the 14th of April 2020. Yesterday we were advised by our visa agents that we could only apply for our main spousal visa from the UK if: the countries all stayed in lockdown; the visitor visas had expired or were due to expire. This was not good news for us, as this would delay the application process again and could mean that my family would still have to return to our old country to apply.

It now all depended on this virus. I asked again, 'Please, Jesus, I ask that you make it possible for lockdown to continue in the UK and our old country.' I know at the time it sounded selfish of me to be praying for things to remain in lockdown, but we needed to ensure that travel would not be allowed. This is what we needed to ensure we could stay together while we waited for the visitor visas to expire so that we could do the main visa application from the UK.

Here we are now at the end of April. I was still trying to make plans to get a credit card to make up the money we needed for the visa applications when my mother said she could give us help to pay for them. I didn't really want to take any money from my mother, but at least it was a positive step. Now we had to just wait for a miracle: that my family could remain here and apply for the visa from the UK.

The days were all just rolling in and out. We couldn't go anywhere. Everything was restricted and closed. And we were now in the first week of May 2020. My husband called the airline to ask about his return flight tickets back to our old country; what would happen as they were paid for. But as everything was still in lockdown and travel was still not allowed, they confirmed that all flights at that time were cancelled until July. So we would have to wait until then. But his tickets would still be valid.

By the end of May, our next miracle came and our prayers were answered. The UK changed the dates regarding for applying for visas from the UK to the end of July. This meant that we would be able to apply for the main visas from within the UK and we would stay together as a family while the application was being processed.

A day later and even better news came; as we were now able to apply for the main visa within the UK, the costs were lower. HOW GREAT IS OUR GOD! Thank you, Lord, thank you, Jesus, for answering our prayers. We were so happy, and it felt like a load was lifted from our shoulders. The happiness and excitement that we could apply for the visas within the UK (and that the costs would be cheaper) was all demolished in a second. A day later, we found out that because the children's visas had been reissued as a result of the mistake that had been made, the expiry date on their visas was now August. So here we were again, stressed and worried as everything had to be placed on hold again, with the suggestion that they might have to go back to our old country to do the applications, and being hurt. Again it seems the devil is trying to get to us; just as we get good news, he comes in and ruins everything.

I had to keep telling myself, 'God has brought us this far. He has already made so many different things happen to get us to this point. I know it has not been easy and some parts almost ripped me to pieces, but for now, we were safe and together as a family.' I knew that God would work his wonders again and answer our prayers. We just had to keep believing, having faith to know he is there with us and working on things.

God has answered our prayers again. A few days later we were advised that things have changed again and we could now apply for the spousal visas. Finally! The day we had been hoping and praying for was finally here. On the 4th of June 2020 we submitted our applications for the main spousal visas, and everything was now paid for.

There were a few things that were making me worried, such as had we completed everything correctly, what would happen if they didn't get the visas? But as quickly as these thoughts came into my head, I would pray and hand the negative thoughts over to Jesus and ask Him to please keep working on our application, as this was all in his control. He was the only one that could work on situations with the application.

Jesus had made it possible for us to submit the visas from the UK. He even helped us with our finances—everything was cheaper as we were applying from within the UK. It was all in God's hands and we just had to continue our walk with Him in faith and trust that everything would work out.

On the 18th of July we received an update on the visa submission. It was not actually at the submission stage yet; there were additional details needed. One was that my husband had to do an English test. We had tried to book an appointment as soon as possible, but due to lockdowns and everything not working at full speed, there were delays, and his appointment could only be done at the end of July. But I knew it would all work out and be okay. We just had to stay positive and keep our faith.

While everything was delayed and slow, it was not a nice feeling and at times we felt frustrated, but the positive side was that we were still together as a family. If they had been back in our country, not have been permitted to stay in the UK, these delays would have been heartbreaking, and I don't think I would have been able cope, but thank the Lord I didn't have to.

We are now almost at the end of June and we are no closer to submitting, and a strange thing has happened with my daughter. She seems to have stopped eating and her stomach is giving her trouble. With doctors not being very helpful in this time I didn't know what to do, or how to help her. Again I had to turn to God, to tell Him that the devil was trying to get us down again and affect us in a different way. I handed my daughter's health over to him and asked that he please help her with whatever was going on.

Another month later and we had to travel to Birmingham, as my husband had to take an English test at a specific examination centre there. I was waiting in the car and praying that God would be with him, help him to stay calm and help him to pass the test. At the same time I felt or knew that he would be fine. This was a test to see if you could speak and understand English. He was obviously fine with this—better than a lot of people I had spoken to recently who are not from the UK.

Once he had finished, we had to start the trip home. But here we go again; the car made a huge noise. Something was not right. We were far from home, and we didn't really know what to do. The noise was terrible, but the car seemed to still drive okay, so we took the chance and kept going. All the way home I was praying and praying to Jesus that He would just keep the car going until we got back home. And after 3 hours, we made it back home safely. THANK YOU, LORD.

It seems odd that every day, week or month something keeps happening that makes things worse, then I have to ask God for help. I always think to myself that there are so many other people out there with much bigger and worse things happening in their lives that they need help with, and I don't want to keep bothering God with my issues and problems, but at the same time I know that in the Bible it says that we should do this, as He will lighten our burdens, and that we should lay it all down at the cross for Him. But I still felt guilty asking all the time.

Today was the 30th of July and we got the great news that my husband had passed his English test. More good news was that they have extended the date for people to apply for visas within the country to the end of August. This finally means that the worry that my family may still have to leave to complete the visa applications is no longer a worry. We can stay together as a family and do everything from within the UK. THANK YOU, LORD, again for your miracles, and for answering our prayers.

Unfortunately, as one worry ended, another was still there: the car we had was now a problem. The garages could not work out what the problem was, so we would now have to sell it and get a newer car. This was an additional cost we couldn't really afford. We knew that the condition of our current car meant we would not get much for it, but my husband took some time looking around on the internet to see if he could find something that would hopefully be in a better condition than our current car but not be expensive.

Thank you to Jesus for making it possible for us to apply for the visas in the UK, that we didn't have to pay the higher visa costs, which left us a little extra money to put towards a replacement car.

Things always seem to work out in an odd way, don't they? One minute you think you have no money, then things change, and you think, great, now I have some extra money. But then just after this, something else happens and guess what, that extra money you thought you had, now must be used to pay for something else.

I always see these situations as being like a battle between good and evil. When times are hard and we believe God will help us, God answers and helps. But the devil knows that as God helps us, our faith and love and trust in God grows more, so the devil swoops in and then tries to do something to turn things around in a negative way to affect us. And this can sometimes break our trust, faith and love for God. It's just a vicious circle with no end.

However, my family and I have been through enough over the years that I do know, no matter how bad things look, even when there seems to be no light at the end of a very long tunnel, that God will always be with us, and He will never leave us. The Bible tells us this, and the dream I spoke about earlier in the book tells me that it's true, no matter how hard things may seem.

We were now halfway through September 2020 and there was no update or word on the main visas for the children and my husband. I also feel as if Jesus has forgotten us. No matter how hard we pray, nothing is happening, nothing is changing, and we just feel stuck in limbo. However, at the same time, I do know that Jesus is there and still with us. I don't really like this job I'm in now, but I pray every day that He can help me with my work. Then things do happen throughout the day. That lets me know it was Jesus helping me. All I could keep doing was pray that the Lord, King of Kings, would hear our prayers on the visas, and help us move forward.

Due to the whole Covid situation still having so many restrictions about not leaving your homes, everyone in our household was starting to get frustrated. We couldn't really get out much as most places were closed on and off. And restrictions applied. And my husband just wanted to start working. I really wished I could get the children registered at a school, but we couldn't do anything without the visas.

Believe it or not the next day, late in the evening, we finally received an email from the Home Office, that we could upload all our final documents for the visas. My husband spent the next few days getting all the documents and information together and finally on the 18th of September 2020 we submitted the last details for the visas. Thank you, Jesus, thank you Lord for everything you have done, and thank you for everything you are still going to do for us.

We were now in November 2020. Last week our visa company gave us an update that the family who applied just before us had received their visas. Here in the UK we were worried as we were going into another month of lockdown because of Covid.

I prayed to God again and asked that he please hear my prayers and that we would get our visas before going into lockdown, which was only a week away.

Four days later, the 6th of November 2020, my husband called me to the kitchen early in the morning while we were making coffee. He took a big breath and said, 'Guess what?' And he paused and went on to say that our visas had been approved. For a moment I thought he was just joking (as he's a big joker), but then he showed me. There on his phone was the long-awaited email showing the letter of approval from the Home Office.

Here we were, just over a year ago we'd started this journey to the UK, and three months in I thought I would not make it through. But here we are now. We have our own place to live, we stayed together as a family through the visa application, our finances have just made it through, and we now had the visas.

I immediately had to say thank you, Jesus, thank you Lord. Thank you for everything that He had done to bring us to this point, to the end of this long and hard chapter in our lives. It was a long hard journey to get to this day, but here we were. Finally we had the visas. Now we could start our next journey and chapter in our lives, to settle down and make a start to our new lives here in the UK.

The spousal and dependent visas take a total of 5 years. Through these 5 years, you get the first visa, which we now finally had, but this is only valid for two and a half years. After this you have to apply for an extension for another two and a half years. After the 5 years, you have to do a year on a leave to remain visa. It is only after this that you can apply for British citizenship. So while we had reached this first point, we still had a long way to go. But for now we were just happy that we had reached this point of getting the first set of visas, and that our lives here in the UK could finally move on. My husband could start working and the children could finally go to school and the stress and worries could be lifted for now.

New Beginnings

As we now had the approval letter, we started the process to get the children into school. For my daughter this was going to be hard; she still missed her old school and friends and she had not been in education for over a year now. All she was used to was being home schooled.

For my son this would be his first time going to school, so this would be a big step for him too. You might remember he didn't ever go to nursery school back in our country as it was too expensive for us at the time and we couldn't afford it. So he was also only used to being at home and not confident really being around other children or people.

In the application process we had to complete details of our school choices. You had to list three schools in order of preference. One school was really close to where we lived, so this is the school we put down as our first choice. It was within walking distance and everyone we had spoken to said it was a very good school. We hoped they would have space for both our children.

My husband called the school directly and ask if they had any openings for the years our children were to be in, but the receptionist just said that the school was full, and they had no spaces available. Here we were again. Sorry, God, I thought you had just helped us reach a point in our lives where I wouldn't have to pray and ask for help every day, but here I was praying again that He would help make it possible for our children to go to this school if it was best for them. The lady who assisted us with the school applications advised that it would take about a week to approach the schools. She would then give us a call to confirm which school the children would be going to.

On that Friday my husband and I were on our way to the shop when his phone rang. As he was driving and we didn't have a car with a phone system fitted I answered the call. There was a man on the line who said he was from the school we'd put down as our first choice. He paused before confirming that both children had been accepted by the school and they could start the following Monday. Thank you, Jesus, thank you Lord. You are great! You have heard and answered our prayers again.

Today was now the 16th of November 2020, the first day of school for the children. They were a little nervous but excited at the same time. Because of Covid we were not able to go into the school with the children, but they seemed to be fine going with the teachers.

After dropping them off I had to get back home to do an exam online, as I had to get a new qualification to remain in my current job. It was stressful, as it took for ever to get into the testing system and take the exam. I just kept praying throughout the exam for God to please help me as I needed to do well and pass. (I needed to do this exam and three more to keep my job.)

The exam was multiple choice, and you had to have a camera on you at all times, as there was someone watching you the other end to ensure you didn't cheat.

Once I'd had finished the exam, it flashed up to say that I had passed. How great was that! Thank you, Lord, for helping me with this first exam.

When the children got home that afternoon, they said they'd had a good day and enjoyed it.

The next few months just rolled on by and we are now at the end of February 2021. Christmas was not that nice, as we didn't have much money to make it fun for the children, and in January we were in full lockdown again due to Covid.

My husband's visa card finally arrived, meaning that now hopefully our lives could move forward and he could start working. But it would be hard to find work at this time, as most companies were not fully open nor functioning properly due to Covid and lockdowns.

I know that it may sound as if Covid was holding us back now in a different way than before. I knew that many people where losing their lives and it was ripping families apart, so at the same time I was thankful that the children were now able to do online schooling (due to the lockdowns), and my company let us continue to work from home. This meant that we could stay safe during the hard times of Covid, which just seemed to be getting worse at times and seemed never ending.

We now jump to the start of April 2021. It has taken some time, but my husband has finally been offered a job. It is on a contract basis, but a job was a job at that moment, and something was better than nothing.

However just as quickly as the job offer came, a problem has arisen. The company said that he should have already applied for his UK driver's licence. We tried to explain that due to a delay in receiving his visa card we were unable to apply for it, but they then turned around and said that he could not work for them, as a UK licence was necessary. This was not a nice feeling for my husband; the first opportunity that came up and it disappeared just as quickly.

'Lord, please, I hand this over to you,' I prayed. 'Please can you help my husband find a job. He is getting depressed not being able to work, just sitting at home all the time.' Being unable to contribute to all the costs was really starting to frustrate him.

By the end of April my husband was contacted by his brother-in-law, who had his own company. He offered him a job on a contract basis. This also meant that he would have to work away from home again, but this time it was not out of the country like all his previous jobs; it was just in another city, which meant that he could come home at the weekends. Thank you, Lord, for giving my husband this opportunity. I'm sure this will open more doors for him in the UK job market, as this seems to be a big issue if you don't have experience working in the UK.

I had the same problem when I first came over to the UK looking for work: no one wanted to give me a job as I hadn't worked in the UK before (which all seemed a little odd to me). If no one gave you an opportunity to work, how would you ever get a job? I'd always thought it was just an easy way out to say no instead of saying directly that they didn't want foreigners working for them.

For now everything seemed to settle down. We were both working now, and we felt better that we could keep moving forward. My husband's contract was to come to an end in June, however it seemed the company was happy with the work they were doing and it has been confirmed that their contracts will be extended for another three months, so this was a relief again. Thank you Lord.

It is really not nice having a contract job. Yes, it might pay well, but the uncertainty is always there around when the project will finish and it's always at the last minute you learn whether the contract will be extended. You can never take on a new contract because you're not sure what is happening with the current one, so it is just very stressful.

My husband is also a little stressed by what he is doing. His work was always on mines, but now the work he was doing was in a warehouse and while he was doing work that he'd always wanted to learn, it was stressful as he had to learn on the job. And while he enjoyed most days, there were also some that were hard for him, as he was not always sure what to do, and he didn't like not being sure of his work.

We also heard today that my husband's mother has Covid. This was another worry for my husband. Her lungs had not been very strong for years before this and now with the Covid she had a hard time breathing, but she seemed to be okay. In the place where she lived, they were keeping an eye on her (they'd already lost a few people in the care home to the virus).

I had been going for treatment for my psoriatic arthritis. The medication they had me on was making me feel sicker every day and I had to inject myself once a week. The medication was also used for people who were undergoing chemo. I had been on this medicine for a while now. They start you off on a low dose, then increase it until you reach the full dosage, depending on your situation. As my condition was very bad, I had to have the highest dose, but it just made me feel worse and worse. The doctors just said it was normal when I complained.

Once I reached the full dose, they said my system would settle and then I should feel better. During this time my psoriasis and arthritis were so much better, and I hardly had pain. But even though my skin started to look normal, I wished that I could also feel better.

After being on the full dose for a few months my system just didn't seem to settle down. I was still feeling sick all the time. And feeling sick was worse than having the pain. I felt like I couldn't move around some days because my head would spin so much that I would get dizzy. This meant that I would have to sit still all day, otherwise I felt sick all the time. I would be sleeping or lying down in bed, and everything would be spinning. I would then have to try get to the bathroom to be sick. This was starting to become worse and worse, and it was very hard for me at work. I just couldn't take it anymore, so I asked that my medication be changed. The doctors didn't want to change my medication, no matter how I was feeling. They said it was the best medication for me to be on and if I changed to another medication, it was not half as good and worked much slower, meaning that my skin would worsen again and so would my arthritis. So they insisted that they wouldn't change my medication.

We have now moved on to the end of July 2021. My husband is not very happy with working away anymore. The driving up and down is getting to him now. The trip should only take about four to five hours, but heavy traffic and accidents could increase this to seven or more hours before he would make it home. Then he would be so tired from driving up on the Friday that on the Saturday he didn't really want to do anything. Then on the Sunday he wouldn't want to drive or do much again as he knew he had to leave early Monday morning to be at work by 9 am. But for now we knew that at least he had a job and that things would change. We just had to hang in there.

This is where I kept going back to the Bible verse that God gave us before I left our country: Jeremiah 29:11.

'I know the plans I have for you, says the Lord. 'They are plans to prosper you and not to harm you, plans to give you hope and a future.' (New King James Version)

I know things will get better we just have to keep believing and praying.

We have had some good news today. My husband's mother seems finally to be getting better after having Covid. It has taken her a while, but we are just thankful that she is finally recovering now.

A few months later and December 2021 was coming up fast. The days and months just seem to be flying past now, but the bad news was that my husband's contract would come to an end that month. Because of the time of year and places still not working to full capacity due to Covid, there was no contract extension this time and no new jobs in the pipeline.

Already Another New Year

Yes, here we were now in 2022. My word, how time flies! Over Christmas our car broke down and we can't drive it now as my husband has no work. *And* we can't afford to fix it. Yes, the stress starts all over again, as by the end of this year we have to start the whole process of extending the spousal visas. This means that we will need a lot of money again, and this time I have no idea how we are going to get it together. It's in God's hands.

Things here are really hard. Back in our old country there were many more things around, like billboards, verses on trucks and cars, to give you a little boost to remind you that God is around, some inspiration and a comforting word to show that you are not alone. However, here in the UK where we live, there is nothing: not a sign nor a car showing any religious verses, nothing around to pick you up a little when you are feeling down or losing hope. All I can do is pray that this will be a good year for us, that my husband will get a good job and that our children will settle in so that we can start living our lives and be happy again.

Have you ever thought about the last time you laughed? I don't mean the fake ha-ha, that's funny kind, I mean the genuine joy where you can't help but laugh, and you can't stop; you laugh so much that you get tears in your eyes. I miss that feeling of pure happiness, even if it is temporary.

The days just seem to roll into one with the same routine: wake up, get the children to school, go to work, come home, have dinner, get everyone to bed and sleep. It all just keeps going round and round every day. There is no change.

The treatment for my psoriasis was also now really getting me down. I couldn't bear feeling sick all the time, so I complained to the doctors again. Finally, they listened and changed my medication. The best part was, I didn't have to inject myself once a week anymore; I just had to take pills, which I thought would be so much better.

Within about two weeks I was feeling better. Yes, my skin psoriasis had been getting worse again—quickly—and so were my aches and pains, but I felt so much better. I could do things without wanting to constantly be sick.

In June 2022, three months after changing my medication, one morning I woke up and saw that my skin had some other marks on it. They looked almost like little blisters, but as they didn't look like anything serious, I just left it and thought that maybe something had bitten me.

A few days later it spread and things got really bad and ugly quickly. The little blisters became huge and I was itchy all over and coming out in big red swollen welts. I called the doctor (they weren't seeing patients face to face at the time because of Covid) and they said that I should wait a few days but treat the condition with antihistamine from the chemist. They said this should help.

However, by the next day there was a new outbreak on my neck. I thought to myself, *NO, I must insist on seeing a doctor*. I didn't want whatever this was to move onto my face, because I knew that whatever happened with my skin could change into psoriasis. So I called the doctor and insisted they see me urgently. Things got bad quickly in a day. My whole body was now covered in this huge rash and swollen red areas. It looked terrible. The doctor advised that I stop all medication as he thought it might have been an allergic reaction to the new medication. I asked how that could be. I'd been on the new medication for a few months already and reached the maximum dose over a month ago. How could I have an allergic reaction only now? But they insisted it must be, so I had to stop all medication, and they gave me a strong antihistamine and antibiotics to try and stop the reaction. Then they made an emergency appointment for me with a dermatologist to see if they were correct and to ensure there was nothing else going on.

I got to see the dermatologist three days later. By this time the rash had gone, the swelling had gone down and there were only a few blisters left, but everywhere the rash had been had now changed into psoriasis, so I went from having not much psoriasis on my body back to having it all over again. And this time it was ten times worse—and sore. My body was now 90 per cent covered with psoriasis.

For people who don't know what this condition is, it is an immune system disorder that causes your body to go into overdrive. And it makes layers and layers of skin. Depending on how bad your case is, it can be extremely painful. A person's skin stays dry, no matter what you put on. Even Vaseline doesn't moisturise it. When you move, your skin cracks from being so dry and your skin rips apart and starts to bleed. Your skin is so itchy that you feel like you have lots of bugs crawling all over you, but if you scratch or rub your skin, it's extremely painful. To make it just that little bit worse, the skin is so dry that whenever you move you leave what looks like a snowstorm where you sitting or standing. It is a terrible disease to have and very embarrassing as there is nothing you can do to stop it.

The dermatologist didn't want to put me on any more medication until my system had recuperated from the bad reaction, so I just stayed on the antihistamines, and she provided me with cream to try and make things better.

After about a month, I went back to the dermatologist as they'd stopped the strong antihistamines and I couldn't take the itchiness anymore. The doctor gave me another month's supply and said that owing to the severity of my condition I would be put on a list for some other treatment options. However, that would mean injections again, and I would have to be monitored through the process. To be honest I didn't want any repeat of that feeling sick business again, nor the possibility of having another allergic reaction, but my skin and pain was so bad that I agreed they could put my name down.

As it could take a long time to get these new treatments started, the doctor said she would start me on UV treatment to help with the psoriasis on my skin, which was so bad. I had to go for UV treatments twice a week as they start you on low doses and increase the amount every time you go. While it seemed to work in one way, in another way it dried out my skin even more, and this made the itch and my snowstorms of skin worse. Every time I moved, I would leave behind a white blanket of skin. Our house looked terrible. I would sweep and vacuum every day, but within an hour, or particularly after a bath, the carpets and floors were white. It may sound like an overexaggeration but it's not. It was terrible and very embarrassing and I hated it. At work it was even worse; I could only wear long clothes to try and cover everything up, so I wore long knee-high socks to try and reduce the amounts of skin I would leave on the floor. But you could still see it and my chair would be covered. I would try and not move too much, and if I got up, I would give my chair a quick wipe to get the worst skin off, but there was nothing I could do to make things better or lose less skin.

Before you ask or wonder, I'd had psoriasis from the age of thirteen. It started off in my hair and as I got older, my skin got worse, and in my late twenties the arthritis started. I had been praying for years to be healed and had tried all types of treatments, but unfortunately this prayer was never answered. This whole situation had just got to a point where I didn't want to go anywhere or do anything as I couldn't handle my skin and pain.

While all this was happening to me, my husband got news that his mother was not doing very well again. This was a worrying time for my husband, as he knew that his mum had not been well for some time, and things seemed to be getting worse for her. But he spoke to her and she said she was okay and seeing the doctors.

His younger sister confirmed that she was not well and they were trying to figure out what was going on.

Around this time we saw that there would be a large prayer meeting happening in September 2022, back in our home country, for people to pray about general problems and heal people. This was being arranged by a local pastor. My husband suggested that we should go to this gathering; he just felt that we should go.

I said no to going. I was in no state to travel and we didn't have the money to spend on this, as the flights were expensive. But on the other hand, if we did go, he would get to see his mother and other family members, whom we'd not seen for years, so I felt bad for saying no.

During the month of August, my mother-in-law's health seemed to be getting worse. She was going to see the doctors and they were doing tests to discover what the problem was. Through all this she said she was generally okay; she just didn't feel very good on some days.

I said to my husband that maybe he should fly over to see if he could help her, but his response was, what could he do, they were running tests, and his mother didn't seem to be worried. His younger sister didn't seem too concerned about it either. However, as the days passed her health deteriorated even more and they admitted her to hospital. After my husband had spoken to his mother to find out what was going on, he said she sounded fine; she'd just said she was not feeling very well.

Unfortunately, only a few days later in early September she passed away. It was so unexpected. She was fine one day and by the next morning she had passed. This was terrible for us all—and heartbreaking. My husband was broken as we'd looked at tickets for him to fly out just the night before she passed away, and now it was too late. We were all heartbroken, but we had to continue buying flights to head back to our country. Unfortunately, it was now due to sad circumstances.

We didn't have a lot of spare money as we were saving for our visa costs which was coming up soon. But owing to the situation we would now have to use these savings to pay for the travel costs and other things in between. No matter what we did, only one specific week in September had the cheapest flights. My husband's older sister also said it was only this specific week that they could get affordable flights for her and her daughter. We couldn't afford to take our children with us; the price of flights was just ridiculous.

At the same time my husband and his older sister were trying to help their younger sister and brother with arranging the funeral back in our old country. With our dates of travel confirmed they could now start the final arrangements.

While all this was happening, we totally forgot about the prayer meeting, which my husband had originally wanted to attend. Then one day my husband's older sister said that the friend they would be staying with (when they were over for the funeral) would be going to the meeting on the Saturday because she was helping out with the event. She asked if we wanted to go with them. While it seemed wrong to go to the prayer meeting while we were there for their mother's funeral, every one of us had this feeling that we had to go.

So we all agreed that we would go to the meeting. The time would be rushed, but these were the only dates that made the trip affordable for us all. Also, most of this time would be spent travelling, but we knew we could squeeze in everything that needed to be done before having to return back to work.

It worked out that we would be away for a week. While all the arrangements were being made, we learnt I had a problem with my South African bank account. Someone had paid in a large amount of money in and was now having debits taken off my account. I tried to get this sorted over the phone, but just as I would start explaining, the call would get cut off. It cost a fortune to call back every time, so I also planned to go to the bank when we were there to get things sorted.

My husband and I would leave Carlisle and drive down to his older sister in Peterborough on the Tuesday. We would then leave the UK on the Wednesday evening, landing back in South Africa on the Thursday morning.

When we landed, we went straight to the bank, hoping it would be a quick thing to get sorted. However, it took from just after 10 am that morning to just after 3 pm to get things sorted. We came to realise that I'd been a victim of identity theft, so we had to call and notify all the banks involved and I was just so grateful that it could all be sorted; it was one less thing to worry about. After this we headed off to drop my husband's older sister and daughter off at the place they would be staying.

The following day we had to go and pick them up again. We were staying at opposite ends of the city, so it took a good hour to get to them from where we were staying at the time. We had to go over to their cousin's house too, which was also at the opposite end of the city and about another hour's drive. This was to say hello and arrange what we would all be doing on the Sunday for the funeral service, and how we would all be getting there. After visiting and making the final travel arrangements, we then headed back to our place, having first dropped off his older sister again.

The next day was the prayer meeting that we had planned to go to, and we had to be up early and get moving as this was again about hour's drive from where we were staying. As we were driving along, we didn't know where we were going. All we knew was that is was somewhere in an open area in which there was a small mountain on the top of which a large white cross had been erected. However, we needn't have worried because as we got closer to the place we saw flags and people showing the way. The feeling that came over us as we drove along seeing these people was so uplifting and strange that it actually made me just want to cry. There were more and more people as we drove along the dusty path. Everyone was happy, smiling and saying hello, there was not one cloud in the sky and everything felt peaceful and exciting at the same time.

We eventually found a place to park, as it was a walk to the main area. Looking around and hearing all the people talking, and seeing this huge white cross, made me think how great it was that so many people could come together to hear the word of God. Eventually we found my husband's older sister as she had travelled with the other people they were staying with. The morning air was crisp and fresh with a little chill.

Now it is important for me to tell you that my husband also had a younger brother. Unfortunately, he had lost his way with drugs and alcohol, but the people at the place where he was staying were bringing him to the prayer meeting. My husband felt so bad for him. It was his younger brother and all he wanted to do was help him, but he also felt lost as there was not much he could do to help.

Before the prayer meeting started, they were playing some of the most wonderful Christian music. With every song that played you could feel this wonderful power going through you. The music was loud, but at the same time it gave me a comforting feeling. It was so amazing to see hundreds of people walking down the hills and coming from every direction to come together.

My husband's younger brother found us and sat with us. After a while, they went off for a walk and a chat. Sitting there listening to the music, I felt that my husband had been wrong; we were meant to come to this meeting, but I didn't think it was for healing my psoriasis. I think it was for his younger brother.

The prayer meeting began. The sun was now very hot shining down on us. Now and again there would be a nice cool breeze that would blow and cool everyone down just a little.

There were a lot of things said through the service that touched me and made me think. As the meeting was coming to an end and they were going to pray for healing, there was still a huge part of me that wanted that miracle, to look down at my arm and not see any psoriasis, only normal skin.

As they started praying for healing. The preacher said, 'During this time you need to leave people and let things happen.' The nice cool wind seemed to have disappeared and it was hot. There was not one cloud in the sky, and the heat was becoming really bad. People started to feel the clothes on their skin get really hot. As I had psoriasis, I had to wear long sleeves, so it made it feel even worse, but we stood and prayed.

After the one prayer I started to feel ill. I tried to act as if I was okay, but I was feeling very dizzy and faint. So I sat down and had something to drink. As I sat, I looked around. Maybe I was feeling this funny as I was being healed. I looked at everyone to make sure no one was looking at me and I moved my sleeve slightly. As I looked down, I realised I was not healed. I felt a little disappointed as I knew then it was just the heat that was getting to me.

The meeting ended and we had to pack up and leave, and I was not feeling well at all. My head was spinning and I was feeling extremely sick. I would walk a few steps and then have to stop. Eventually we got to the car. I just sat still and had to roll up my sleeves, my husband had put the aircon on full power to cool the car down, but as it had been baking in the sun all day, it was taking a long time. We also had to try and find his older sister, but this was not easy. We had stopped on one side of the mountain and they had stopped on the other side. So we just had to drive in the general direction they were in. However, after a few calls and driving and waiting, we all met up again, then headed back to their cousin's house.

When I spoke to my husband's older sister a little later that evening, she said that when we were at the prayer meeting she wanted to tell me that not all healing happens quickly; some healing takes a longer time. I knew then that I just had to be patient and that my healing would eventually come.

The following day was the funeral service. This was a sad day for everyone and a hard day to get through.

Our trip back to the UK was not as smooth as we'd hoped. When we arrived at the airport at about 5 pm, we saw that our flight was delayed, and they would not let us book in. Eventually, we were told that the flight was cancelled due to a problem with the plane. Then we were told that we would be taken to a hotel and advised of flight details the next day. What a mess this was!

At about 11 pm that night, all the people from the flight were put onto buses. We were then driven to a hotel where everyone was told to get off. We stood in a long queue and waited for about an hour. When we were almost at the front desk, we were advised that the hotel was full and we were told to get back on the buses to go to another hotel. Everyone was very irritated by this time. This was not organised well at all. Why on earth would they not call ahead and book say a hundred people into one hotel and then take only those people to that hotel.

We arrived at the next hotel and once again had to stand in a queue, waiting and moving forward slowly. As before, after about an hour, we were getting close to the front, and people were beginning to learn that this hotel was nearly full. But thankfully, we did make it to the front and were booked in. Finally, at about 2 am we were in our room and could finally get some sleep. We had been advised that we had to check out by 10 am that morning.

All the passengers were given breakfast, and then everyone had to sit in the reception area and wait to be advised about what was going to happen. Some people were advised early that they had been put on other flights. After hours of sitting, we were eventually informed that my husband and I were to be put on a flight to the UK via Zurich. However, his sister and her daughter were not told anything. The airline had not arranged any transport to get back to the airport, so we had to get our own taxi and left the hotel at about 3 pm that afternoon. That night we got on our flight and finally started our trip home.

All I can say about that experience is that for a huge well-known airline, I would have thought that they would have excellent contingency plans in the event of problems. But as we found out, they didn't, and that just made everything so stressful and much harder for all the passengers.

The morning we landed in the UK, we had to try and find a different train back to Peterborough, as all our travel arrangements had been messed up due to the day's delay. The train company was not willing to assist us with the original travel arrangements that we'd booked, saying it was not their fault that we'd been delayed.

At this time my mother called to say that our son had been very sick through the night, so all I wanted to do was get home. But I knew it would be a long day ahead with travelling, so all I could do was say that we were on our way but would be there much later that night.

We eventually found a train heading back to Peterborough, and it would be leaving five minutes later, so here we were now running from one side of the train station to the other to try and make it to the train (the cost for the next train would have been over a hundred pounds, which was just a huge amount to pay).

We finally arrived in Peterborough, and now we had to try and get back to his sister's house, which was almost an hour's drive away. We could have taken a bus, but this would have been so much more of an issue as we had to wait for the right bus, and change buses again later. And buses take too long as they stop all the time. My husband was so tired and irritated by this time that he said we would get a taxi and pay the amount just to get there quicker without the worry of long bus journeys and stops.

We finally made it back to his sister's house. Originally the plan had been to spend the night and travel the next day, however as we were now a day behind and my son was ill, we just loaded up our car and started the five-hour drive back home.

In the days that followed my psoriasis seemed to get even worse again, and I had to start the UV treatments again starting with a low dose. From there things continued as before; every day just went back into one blur: wake up, go to work, children to school. Nothing much changed and we had the worry about the visas costs that were coming up the following year.

Coming to an End

Christmas came and went. It felt like a blink of an eye and here we were now in 2023.

This was the year that we had to apply for the spousal visa extension for my husband and children. As we had used most of our visa money for the trip back to our country, we were not sure how we were going to afford the costs, but at the same time knew that God would help us.

Over the previous few months, we had also enquired about our children being in the country for three years because we'd heard and read that if children had been in the UK for a continuous three years with no breaks, they could qualify for British citizenship. If our children did qualify, this meant we would not have to do the visa extensions and the costs would come to an end quicker. If they didn't qualify for the citizenship route, we would have to do the two-and-a-half-year visa extension, then after this, the indefinite leave to remain for a year. Only then could we apply for citizenship. This would be three and a half years and large costs, but if they could apply to get citizenship now, it would just be one more large cost and then the children would be sorted.

We asked our agent about this citizenship route for the children, and she investigated the matter for us. After discussing with solicitors, she came back and confirmed that as the children had been in the UK for three continuous years they would qualify for this route. We were so grateful for this news. Once again while Covid had been a terrible time, it had been a blessing for us, as the children and my husband were unable to leave the UK during lockdown. Not only that, not being able to afford to take the children with us to my mother-in-law's funeral had made it possible for us to apply for their citizenship (as their residency had not been interrupted).

Once again, how great is our God! Even when we don't understand things at times, God knows best and is working on different situations even when at the time we don't know why things are happening.

In the first week of March 2023 we were able to apply for British citizenship for our children, and while everyone was confident that there would be no problems, I must admit I had a little doubt, which I knew was wrong. I tried to ignore it and I had to pray about it, as I knew that it was in God's hands and that he would not have helped us to find this route if it wasn't going to work. I couldn't see how God would bring us this far to only now make things fall apart, as we knew that if this application didn't work, we couldn't afford to pay the additional amounts to extend their current visas. And we didn't even know if they would let us do an extension if the citizenship was not accepted, as everything would happen at the same time.

We wanted to hear back about the children's citizenship application before we submitted my husband's visa extension, however time was running out. (Although to be honest we needed the extra time to try get the money together for his application.) However, it came to a point where we could no longer wait; we had to submit the application for my husband's visa extension (by this time we had just got enough money together to pay for his application).

Here we were again. Everything was in the air: the uncertainty, the worry and the endless waiting where time seems to drag on. All we could do was check emails all day, or wait for the phone to ring, to get an update on the applications.

After about a month of waiting, we knew that it was coming close to when we should receive news about the children's applications. However, the estimated day came and went, and we had no communications or updates. Whenever you do any application, it always states that you may have to wait between 4 weeks to 8 weeks. But it could also take months depending on each individual application.

The days kept passing and I was getting a little worried. The children's current visas would run out in May and I was starting to worry about what would happen if the outcome on the citizen application was unsuccessful. I just had to keep praying and telling myself that no matter what the outcome was, we would be okay, as God would be there with us.

Then on the 21st of April 2023 I was working from home and my phone rang. It was the lady from the agency we'd used for the applications. She said, 'Hi I'm just calling to let you know that they have heard from the Home Office about the children's applications.' She paused and then said, 'Congratulations, the children have obtained their citizenship.'

I was so happy, I thanked her and immediately let my husband know. Wow, what a relief! It felt like a ton had been lifted off my shoulders again. It was fantastic news. After about an hour we then received an email containing a copy of the British certificates for the children. All I could say was thank you, Jesus, thank you, Lord, again for being there in every situation and making this all possible. Now all we had to do was wait for my husband's visa extension. We were sure that there would be no problems with his application; it was just a case of us having to be patient.

In May 2023, my husband finally received confirmation that his visa had been extended. Everything was falling into place again and working out for us.

For now we could take a breath. At the same time we knew that years fly by, and we would be back again two years later when my husband would have to do his application for the indefinite leave to remain. This application would come with its own costs, and other requirements that would need to be met. However for now, we can just take a deep breath, thank Jesus, and worry about the future tomorrow.

With regards to my psoriasis UV treatments, back in April my treatments had come to an end as I'd reached the maximum limit of treatment I could have in a period. In a way I was happy, as I'd thought to some extent the UV treatments had been making the dryness and itching worse. To be honest, throughout the whole treatment process no one even looked at my skin. I would enter the treatment room, they would put on the machine and leave the room. I would stand in the machine for a while, get out, and I would then leave.

When I did complain about my skin being extremely dry and painful, they would just say it was normal and provide me with more creams. All they were ever worried about was if I had been burnt, but that never happened. To be honest, it all seemed like a waste of time. I know that a lot of people have good outcomes with this treatment, but I guess I was not one of the lucky ones.

My husband's older sister had given me a Christian book on healing. It was taking me a long time to read through it, however while reading it, I tried hard to change my mindset and the things in my life that I felt the book was showing me I was doing wrong. When I had finished reading the book, and read more specifically about what causes my disease, it seemed my skin started changing overnight. The itchiness was less and the skin flaking was reducing, the swelling and pain in my joints seemed to get better.

Every day my skin looked better and the pain in my joints was improving. Then one morning I woke up and realised my skin was almost back to normal: hardly any psoriasis anywhere on my skin and I had no pain in any of my joints.

All I could say was thank you Jesus, thank you Lord for answering my prayers, and helping me to see that it was my own sinful thoughts and my own family's history of sins that had been causing my disease. I know this is an ongoing learning experience and I will keep trying to stay on the correct path.

I know you may be reading this and wondering how can an incurable disease just get better, disappear, and all I can say is that for years I prayed for healing and tried all different things, but finally after seeing and realising my mistakes, Jesus healed me. All I can say is, yes, it is a miracle and a blessing from God.

I'd had psoriasis for about 21 years—this was more than half my life. For it to simply go away, with no medicine, no treatments, was a miracle and proof that God does answer prayers. But at the same time, it is all in God's time. And on that path we have to learn to pray, have faith and believe that everything we do affects us daily—and also affects the generations to come.

When I originally started noting details for my book, the first things I made was a list of what I wanted in the future. And God has answered my prayers:

I wanted my daughter to do well at school. She is doing well at school. Even after changing countries and being behind by about 4 years (as the countries work differently), she is coping at school. Thank you, Jesus!

We have come to live in the UK and we are now building our new lives in this country.

My psoriasis and arthritis have left me—inside and out.

My husband is working from home and is with us every day. And he earns a good salary.

I know that through the rest of my life, we will still have hard times that may come and go, that there are still many things that will come in our way when we try to do things, and they will test our faith, but I have also come to learn that we are never alone. No matter what the situation may look like, we are never alone; Jesus is always there with us.

There are many people out there who don't really know God, and this is not always of their own choice but because of how the world is today. I feel so sorry for these people, and for the people who choose to face this world without Jesus.

If people just had a little more understanding of who God is, how Jesus and the Holy Spirit are there for us all, and if they had a little more faith and believed, maybe we wouldn't have so many people who take their own lives, or live with depression because they feel that they can't get out of a bad situation.

I sometimes wish I could just be a little voice saying to each person thinking of making today the end, 'Please! Please! Don't do it. Just hold on, things may seem bad now, and that there is no end in sight, or that there is no need to keep living, but there is! Just hold on! All you need to do is pray. And it doesn't need to be any fancy high English, just speak from the heart, cry if you need to, and pray about your situation and feelings. Ask for forgiveness for all the wrongs you may have done or want to do, and ask for help, peace, love and faith, and your prayers will be heard.

Tomorrow the sun will come up, and even though things may seem the same when you open your eyes, they won't be, because you now have God on your side. He will start working on your situations to make things better for you. All you need to do is just hold on, keep believing, praying and having faith that God is real, that he loves you and that You Are Never Alone.

www.ingramcontent.com/pod-product-compliance
Lightning Source LLC
Chambersburg PA
CBHW060836170426
43192CB00019BA/2799